HOW TO START AND GROW A WILDLY SUCCESSFUL ONLINE BUSINESS

THE SUBSCRIPTION BOX BLUEPRINT

LIAM BRENNAN

Published by: Book Writing Founders
www.bookwritingfounders.co.uk

About the Author

Liam Brennan is an entrepreneur and subscription expert with over 10 years of experience in internet marketing. As the co-founder of BusterBox.com, a successful dog subscription box company with millions in sales and thousands of happy customers across Ireland and the UK, Liam has proven his expertise in building and scaling successful subscription box businesses.

In addition to his work with busterbox.com, Liam is also the founder of Subscription Box Experts, where he shares his tactics and strategies for building successful subscription box companies from scratch. He has helped countless businesses in various niches achieve success through his guidance and support.

In 2017, Liam appeared on Dragons' Den with his business partners and received multiple offers of investment. He is also the founder of the Subscription Box Resources Facebook group, a highly engaged community of new and existing subscription box owners who are all at different stages of their journey.

Currently residing in Dublin, Ireland, Liam can be reached through his website at www.liammichaelbrennan.com or his Subscription Box Resources Facebook Group – www.SubscriptionBoxResources.com.

Listen to his Subscription Box Answers podcast to learn proven tips and strategies about how to start and grow your own successful subscription box business. (You can find it anywhere you listen to podcasts)

Connect with him to learn more about his journey as an entrepreneur and expert in the subscription box industry.

Acknowledgements

I would like to express my gratitude to every single person who has supported me throughout this journey. The time, expertise, and encouragement you have offered are truly invaluable, and I am grateful for the chance to learn from all of you.

Some of you have indirectly impacted my life through your courses, content, and books, despite never having met personally. Others have generously shared their wisdom and advice with me in person, for which I am deeply appreciative.

I would like to specifically extend my appreciation to my girlfriend Racheal and my parents for their unwavering support and motivation. I am also grateful to my business partners, Paul and Gary, for their indispensable contributions to BusterBox. They both played a massive part in everything we accomplished in BusterBox and without them, the company wouldn't have gotten anywhere.

Furthermore, I wish to convey my sincere thanks to Art Raifi and John Stone. Without their guidance and assistance, we would have faced failure long ago. So, thank you.

I would also like to give a warm shoutout to the entire BusterBox team. My gratitude goes out to every staff member, both past and present, who have consistently gone above and beyond for our customers.

Lastly, I want to thank everyone in the Subscription Box Experts Program and the entire Subscription Box community for their dedication to their businesses and for inspiring me to continue learning and growing. Thank you all.

What others are saying

"I've worked with Liam and Buster Box through Subbly for the last 6-7 years and can assertively say he knows how to achieve results with subscription-first business models by following the principles. Liam is a true entrepreneur, and problem solver, and his teachings are practical and fundamentally sound. Get your paper and pen out because this book is going to be packed with advice you need to action right away."

Stefan Pretty. Subbly CEO

"As someone who has been in the subscription box market for close to a decade, I've always admired and trusted Liam as an industry counterpart. As a Co-Founder of Gentleman's Box, I was always looking for other leaders to learn and grow from and during our time launching, scaling, and selling that business, Liam was one of those people. Now at the head of the world's biggest subscription industry event, I continue to value Liam's wisdom.

He is one of the best and brightest minds in the subscription box space. If you're looking for the jumpstart you need in your business, marketing, or in your life, this book will definitely get you there. It's filled with more tactics and strategies than you could ever ask for."

Christopher George, Co-Founder and Chairman, SubSummit

"As one of the Founders of the largest community of subscription leaders in the world, it's always refreshing to come across individuals like Liam. Even after having more than two decades of experience running subscription businesses myself, Liam always finds a way to show me something new and innovative. It's hard to find another individual as driven, motivated, and giving as Liam Brennan. This is why I invite him to speak at SubSummit each and every year. His constant pursuit to helping those around him is abundantly transparent in everything he does and it's extremely evident in this book. The number of actionable take-aways and quality of the advice offered is something ANY entrepreneur or marketer at ANY stage can benefit from."

Paul Chambers, Co-Founder and CEO, Subscription Trade Association

"I've always looked to Liam first for any subscription specific questions I had personally or for the podcast. He's been my biggest mentor, and a massive role model for many more in our industry. Of the hundreds of people, I've had the pleasure to interview for The Subscription Box Show, I don't know of anyone who's had more influence on helping others grow their subscription box businesses than Liam. Not only a personal friend, but in my opinion, the thought leader in the industry. Liam is an exceptional speaker, program creator, coach and now author. I can't wait for you all to discover his genius on paper!"

Eric Musick, Founder and Host of the Subscription Box Show

Table of Contents

CHAPTER 1
The Winning Mindset

It took me a very long time to make any kind of meaningful money online. It felt like I was an out-and-out failure as each business I attempted crashed and burned to the ground. It's hard to believe that I had my first aspiration of making money online when I was sixteen, but it didn't happen for me until I was twenty-six.

Ten years is a very long time to be working on something with not much to show for it. But that was the amount of time it took for me to finally launch a business that started making real money. The funny thing is, though, if I had to do it all over again, I would – a 100%. Why? Because now I know that the journey was worth it. I learned it the hard way; for everything good in life, one has to go through their share of growing to finally be able to achieve their vision.

It was worth it because I ended up selling millions of dollars' worth of subscription boxes, creating multiple successful companies, and ultimately, changing my life completely in the process. When I was getting started though, none of that was ever my goal. All I ever wanted to do was find a way to earn a full-time income online, so I didn't have to work at a regular job anymore.

You might be in the same position yourself right now, and you are dreaming of the day you no longer have to go to your 9 to 5. I am telling you now that this dream is possible, and you can make it a reality.

The internet has completely changed the game and has removed most of the barriers of entry, which stopped people from doing this only twenty years ago. Back in the day, if you wanted to set up your own business, you would have to get a physical location, get a loan from the bank, get stock and take a lot of risks. Nowadays, it is no longer like that at all. You can literally set up a business out of your spare bedroom with little risk and reach customers all over the world.

Though that doesn't mean the journey will be easy. At points, it will be extremely difficult and will feel like there is no end in sight. You may either be at the start of your journey or in the middle of it and struggling, and that is the main reason why I decided to write this book. I want to prove to you that the journey is possible and that you can create an online business which can drastically improve your quality of life once you get it right.

This book is your ultimate guide. I will share with you all my experiences, successes, mistakes and failures, so you can apply that knowledge to your own business and succeed. I will break down the exact path to creating a successful subscription box business and show you that creating a better life for you and your family is possible.

I read a great quote from Mark Cuban a few years ago which said.

"It doesn't matter how many times you fail, you only have to be right once."

This quote really stuck with me, and it's something that I live by. It made me not really care about failure in business at all. I knew it didn't matter how long it took or how many failures I had. All I had to do was get it right once, and then things would all change.

It took me ten years of bouncing around different businesses, losing money, and lots of failures before I really achieved anything. That's the main reason I laugh to myself when I see people giving up and throwing in the towel after a few weeks or months. I find it crazy to think people actually believe they can learn the skills required to build something which will completely change their lives in such a short period of time. It's a very privileged position to be able to earn a full-time income from the comfort of your own home, and if you think you can reach that point without going through some pain first, I am afraid you are sadly mistaken.

I used to think exactly the same way when I was getting started, and I completely underestimated what it would actually take to live life on my own terms. If it was so easy to build a multimillion-dollar business, quit your job and have your dream life, don't you think everybody would be doing it?

The truth is, it's hard! It takes longer than you think to have real success in business, and most people can't handle this. Once reality sinks in, and they realise how difficult it is going to be, they shut down their business and go back to the safety of a job. There is nothing wrong with having a job, either. I know lots of people who work for great companies and are fully satisfied with their nine-to-five routine. Being an entrepreneur is hard, and it isn't something everybody is cut out for or wants to do.

Back in 2009, I was working part-time in a supermarket while studying computer science in college. I still don't know why I thought computer science would be a good idea, but I wasn't happy with my situation at all. I struggled in school with most subjects and ended up getting a very average leaving CERT in the end (The Irish equivalent of a GED). There wasn't a chance I was going to be able to push myself to get a computer science degree, and, truthfully, I wasn't really interested in one either.

I earned a few hundred euros a week in my job and blew that most Friday nights partying. I felt like I was permanently broke, and I couldn't see how I was going to break out of this vicious cycle. I would get paid on Friday, then head out that night partying and be broke again by Saturday morning. My life was becoming a joke. I stopped going to college and ended up leaving after a few months. Now, my life consisted of working part-time in a supermarket and partying with my friends with the little money I earned.

It was a terrible period for me, and I held a lot of resentment towards a previous venture that didn't work out. A year previously, I started importing cars from Japan while I was still in school. The cars that I was importing were very popular and had a very big margin. I was certain that in a few short months, I would have a very lucrative business. My target market was young tradesmen who had plenty of cash and wanted to drive a nice car. What I didn't account for was by the time I ordered the second car, the recession of 2008 had kicked in, and it was nearly impossible to sell anything. The building trade got hit very badly in Ireland, and all the tradesmen lost their jobs.

I felt very sorry for myself back then, and I blamed the government and everybody but myself. I had a nasty victim mentality, and I let the situation drain me to the point I didn't want to bother with business again. See, it is very easy to be passionate about your business when things are going well, but when things get hard, it's much tougher to show up every day and put the work in.

A bad mentality is one of the worst things a new entrepreneur can have, and I see it all the time with new Subscription Box owners. I am in a great situation where I get to work with so many different subscription box owners across every niche possible as private clients, group clients, in my programs or in my subscription box resources community.

I can normally see very quickly if somebody has the right mindset to be successful in business. I used to believe all this stuff about mindset was complete rubbish, but over the last six years, I have come to realise how important it actually is. If you don't have the right mindset, it doesn't make a difference what skills you have, you will not succeed.

This is the mindset you need to be successful

1. You take full accountability for your life

You fully understand and appreciate that you are responsible for how successful you will be in life. You understand that nobody owes you anything, and nobody is going to come and save you. When things go wrong in business, you accept that failure is all part of the game, and you learn from it and improve next time.

Playing the victim is never an option because you know it will get you nowhere. I know this for a fact because I experienced it in my own life. Things never improved for me until I realised this and started taking control of my situation.

2. You're an action taker

You understand that you will never get anywhere unless you are willing to take massive action consistently. The amount of action you will need to take will seem completely unreasonable to most normal people. Your friends and family who work normal jobs may think you have gone crazy. This is what is required to be successful and to build a successful business from the ground up. If you are not ready to commit to this level of action, I wouldn't recommend starting a business.

When we started Buster Box originally, the amount of work we were putting in was insane. We were working full-time jobs and dedicating every other spare minute we had to building the company. I would finish work at 5 PM and then go straight to my business partner's house, and we would work late into the night. Then when it got to the weekend, we weren't out partying and drinking, we were working on the business the whole time.

There were no excuses. We knew what we wanted to achieve would require a big commitment, and we did it. I know everybody's situation is different, but if you aren't willing to commit and put in an enormous amount of effort, do not expect to see any notable results.

3. You appreciate speed

Having the ability to operate at high speed is vital when building a business. It allows you to build up momentum and cut through your problems rapidly. If you are the type of person who sulks when something goes wrong and stops working for long periods of time, you won't be able to achieve anything, and you will always find yourself behind schedule.

When something goes wrong, you should learn from it and then quickly move on to the next idea to try and solve the problem. When you work like this, you solve issues quickly, and it allows you to scale.

I originally learned this was a problem for some people when I started doing 1-on-1 private consulting. Some of the simplest tasks, like installing a tracking pixel or making a slight edit to a website, were taking months to do. This used to frustrate me, and it felt like we were consistently going around in circles on every call. Eventually, I learned some people simply don't have the right mindset or required work ethic to build any kind of business.

Other clients that have gone on to be really successful and build very impressive businesses were the complete opposite. They were taking what I was saying on board and testing things rapidly. If something never worked, it didn't bother them. They knew they had learned something from the experiment and moved on to the next test straight away. These people understood the power of speed, and they were big action takers and eventually achieved a lot of success.

4. You value time

Time is your biggest asset, and you should guard it with your life. This is the one resource that you can never get back. The clock keeps ticking, and once it's gone, it's gone. The best entrepreneurs understand this, and they look for ways to maximise time and make sure they aren't doing unproductive things which waste it.

You will have to do a lot of the heavy lifting yourself in the beginning. This is perfectly normal for any start-up, and you will find yourself and your Co-Founders will be wearing a lot of different hats.

Though you need to realise that this is only temporary, and as you begin to scale up, you will need to hire help. Customer service can take up a lot of time with any Subscription Box business, and it can turn into a serious trap. A lot of founders don't value their time and eventually end up turning into glorified customer support agents in their own businesses.

This is a very poor use of resources and can leave your business in a position where it isn't possible to grow. If you are spending all your time doing customer service, well then, who is going to recruit subscribers and build the company?

It's essential to do customer service at the start, so you understand the biggest issues your customers face and to put strong processes and systems in place. This isn't something you should be doing long-term though. Eventually, you need to hire somebody to take over this job. Then as you get bigger, you should build a team and hire more staff to ensure you are delivering world-class support to your customers.

Another example would be things such as web development and graphic design when you don't have the skills to do the job properly or quickly.

I fell into this trap myself when we initially launched BusterBox. I was determined to design the BusterBox website myself to save money. This was a big mistake because my web development skills were terrible. I spent a few weeks working on it, and it was nowhere near good enough despite all the hours I had wasted. I was getting very frustrated with the amount of time it was taking, and no matter how hard I tried, the site was rubbish-looking.

My business partner eventually convinced me to hire a professional. It worked out very expensive at the time, but it paid off massively and was one of the best decisions we ever made at the start of the business. This is because we ended up launching BusterBox with a website that would convert and make sales

One of the biggest mistakes people make is they try and do everything themselves. They are happy to spend months working on a website that ends up turning out pretty bad and doesn't convert anyway. Or they spend six weeks trying to install a pixel on their website when it would have been much quicker to just hire somebody from Fiverr to do it for you in twenty-four hours.

Obviously, it costs money to hire help, but normally, in the long term, it actually makes you money as you can prioritise your time on things that move the needle forward in your business. If you are the type of person who doesn't value your time and wants to do every single thing yourself, you will not be successful in business. This is because you will waste all your time working in your business and not on your business.

When you are starting your business journey, it is likely you won't have a lot of money, but that still doesn't mean you should do everything yourself. You need to prioritise what you do have and hire people to help with tasks you simply can't do.

5. You view challenges as opportunities

The ability to overcome different challenges and obstacles will be critical to your success. I am afraid there is no way around it, and if you want to build a successful Subscription Box Business, you need to embrace this fact. It does not matter at all how big your business is or where you are in your journey; regular challenges will still occur.

Once we launched BusterBox, one of the biggest challenges was signing up customers.

Then once we figured out how to solve that, churn became a problem. Then once we figured out a way to fight that, hiring the right staff became a problem. The point I am trying to make is there will always be problems. Every single week we have another set of problems that we need to solve. I have lots of friends with many different kinds of businesses, and their lives are exactly the same. This should not scare you. You should embrace this fact and view challenges as opportunities to develop better skills and push your subscription box to the next level.

Your ability to solve problems will reflect exactly how successful your business will be.

Let me give you an example.

If you never manage to solve the problem of getting good at marketing and signing up customers, you won't have any success at all, as a business without customers isn't really a business. Once you do manage to solve your customer acquisition problem, your entire operation will be much stronger. As you can now get the customers, you need to scale and start generating a lot of revenue. The problem happens when you don't view a challenge like this as an opportunity, and instead of trying to solve this problem, you bury your head in the sand.

I see things like this happen all the time. When a big problem comes up, the subscription box owner will bury their head in the sand instead of trying to solve it and start doing some busy body work instead. I hate to break it to you, but just because you are busy doing pointless admin work doesn't mean customers are going to magically start signing up to your subscription box. Forget the admin work and solve the real problem. Then, once the real problem is solved, you will be able to move forward.

Why start with mindset?

Having the right mindset is critical to your success in business. That is why I started the book with this chapter first. If I jumped straight into customer acquisition, churn, or stock control, you would be missing a vital part of the equation.

Having a poor mindset is one of the biggest reasons entrepreneurs fail.

The barriers to entry when setting up a subscription box are pretty low, and that's why the money is in the execution. Think about how many different dog boxes there are. Why is it that most of them barely do any revenue, and a select few have managed to scale into the millions? This is the same across nearly every single niche when it comes to subscription boxes. It is pretty straightforward to get a cardboard box and source some products but making it successful is much more complicated.

The reason a lot of people don't manage to become successful is that they simply don't have the right mindset to cope with all the things they need to overcome. You obviously need to develop your skills and be good at what you do, but that starts with a mindset. When you have a bad mindset, you end up running around in circles and never getting anywhere.

Back in 2015, I experienced two different business failures back to back.

The first company that blew up in my face was a job marketplace website. I thought this was the best idea in the world, and I spent a lot of time and money developing this.

This is how it would work.

- A consumer would post a job listing on the website.
- This could literally be any job at all.
- If you wanted a wall built in your back garden, you could post it.
- If you wanted to hire a DJ for a party, you could post it.
- If you needed some plumbing work done in your house, you could post it.
- My vision was to create a marketplace that would connect consumers to high-quality service providers in the simplest way possible.

- They could check reviews and hire somebody perfect within minutes.
- Each job would be posted into an auction where service providers could bid on it. The consumer could then look at all the bids and reviews and go with the best person possible.
- My company would generate revenue by taking a percentage of the job price.

I thought this would be a highly profitable business; unfortunately for me though, the numbers in the business didn't make sense at all, and it wasn't going to work. I ended up shutting it down after losing a considerable amount of money in the process.

My second business that failed that year was a straight e-Commerce business that focused on men's formal wear.

This failed because we simply couldn't sell enough of the product to make it viable.

I was working full-time during both of these businesses, and when they failed, I decided to go back to college and try to complete my computer science degree. I thought it was getting to the stage where I just had to face facts and get working on a real career. I had tried business many times over and couldn't crack it. It would be better for me to get a degree and settle into a well-paying nine-to-five job. Something didn't feel right to me though, and I regretted my decision as soon as I attended my first lecture.

I vividly remember sitting in the lecture room, dreaming about what my next business would be. I knew I was very close to achieving something, and if I ended up doing this course and continuing to work full-time, I was flushing my dreams down the toilet.

The final nail in the coffin came when I spoke to another student outside the first lecture, and he said this to me.

"This is tough, but in a few years, we will have our degrees, and we can earn €70,000 a year working in a server room."

That was the wake-up call I needed. I was not going to be doing something like that for the rest of my life. The next day I told the college I was leaving and wouldn't be back. My second attempt at a computer science degree was shorter than my first. I only lasted a few hours this time before I quit. My mindset was completely different from before. I knew I was going to set up some form of online business, and this time, it was going to be a success. I started working on BusterBox a few weeks later with my two business partners, and I haven't looked back ever since…

CHAPTER 2
The Subscription Box Business Model

One of the biggest things which attracted me to the subscription box business model was the allure of recurring revenue. I liked the idea of having secure and predictable cash flow coming into the bank account every month. In the past, I had failed with typical e-commerce because I couldn't get the numbers to work or sell enough products consistently. I realised I could prevent both of these scenarios from happening again if I started a Subscription Box.

See, in typical e-commerce, getting the numbers to work in your favour can be challenging if you don't have many different products to sell to your customers. This is because it can be difficult for most niches to make a profit on the first transaction. After subtracting your product, fulfilment, and marketing costs, you will be lucky if you are left with any profit.

To solve this issue, you must ensure you have a good selection of products that you can sell your customers after the first transaction. In many cases, the first transaction is only used to acquire the customer and then repeat business is where you generate your profit.

This is fine in theory and can work, but trust me, it is not easy to build this kind of business. That is why you see thousands of Shopify stores fail all the time. Many new e-commerce entrepreneurs don't realise that it is nearly impossible to generate a profit on the first transaction and don't have any back end built into the business to help them solve this.

I knew setting up a subscription box business would really help with this situation. Moreover, I knew if I had a high customer lifetime value, I would be able to afford to advertise and acquire customers with no issue, and they would still be profitable. I was also well aware of the fact that it did not matter if a customer was profitable immediately on the first transaction because it was a subscription business. The beauty of a subscription business is if you are doing your job right, you will have a high retention rate, and your customers will make a lot of purchases from you and will be very profitable over the lifetime of their subscription.

The other thing that made this business model appealing is that this model allows you a reliable cash flow, making you less worried and pressured to consistently bring in new customers and sales. Obviously, I was going to do everything in my power to grow the company. However, I knew that if we had a bad month of sales, we still had our existing subscribers who were signed up for long-term subscriptions and providing us with the cash flow we needed to pay our bills.

Now, if you aren't familiar with the Subscription Box Business model, don't worry. I am going to use this chapter to explain exactly how it works.

WHAT IS THE SUBSCRIPTION BOX BUSINESS MODEL?

To put it in the simplest way possible, in a Subscription Box Business Model, a customer will sign up for a recurring payment in exchange for a regularly delivered box of products.

The frequency of the payment and delivery could be weekly, monthly, quarterly or yearly. It doesn't make a difference. As long as an automatic recurring charge is built in, then it is a Subscription business model.

Subscriptions are becoming increasingly common as time goes on, and you can find them in all different kinds of businesses. You may be signed up to Spotify for your music or Netflix for entertainment. Or you may be signed up for a selection of different SaaS (Software as a service) products to run your business. Or maybe even a monthly membership that helps you build your business.

The Subscription Box Business model is very similar to how any of these business models work. Instead of music, entertainment, software, or training content, you send a box of products to your customer's door regularly.

As I mentioned earlier in this chapter, the fact that renewals are built into this business model makes it very attractive. You want to build strong connections with your customers and go out of your way to impress them with every delivery. If you do this successfully, your customers will stay subscribed to your subscription box for a long time, and your business will be very profitable.

When you are launching a Subscription Box, you will pick a specific niche. Then every month (or whatever your shipping frequency), you would source a selection of high-quality products, package them together in a box, and deliver them to your customer.

Usually, to improve the experience, each box would have a unique theme. For BusterBox, an example would be the under the sea theme; the box would contain dog toys designed like sea creatures. When you do monthly themes, it keeps things fresh and exciting for your customers and helps improve retention.

Additionally, the Subscription Box Business model is intriguing to customers because they can keep receiving the products they love regularly without the hassle of buying them every month. It's a win-win situation for the business and the customer; I love this model so much.

Once you get to grips with the marketing and have a great box and service, your monthly recurring revenue does not take long to grow significantly.

Let's take a look at an example so I can show you.

- Imagine you charged $60 for your subscription box.
- Your gross margin was 50%, so you earned $30 profit on each box sold.
- With only 500 subscribers, you would be doing $30,000 a month in sales.
- With $15,000 of it as gross profit.

See, it does not take long for your monthly recurring revenue to grow. Through my coaching programs, I have worked with new subscription box owners who have managed to go from 0 to a million-dollar business in just over a year.

That is crazy when you think about it. But it is quite possible with this business model.

This is also a fascinating business model for new entrepreneurs because you do not need much money to start. You can even structure your prelaunch so that you don't pay for any stock until you have sold out, and your customers give you the revenue needed to send the first round of boxes. I will cover a successful prelaunch later in the book, but let me first share how the prelaunch idea works.

Example: Customers Pay For Prelaunch.

- Imagine you were launching a beauty subscription box. You plan to ship your first round of boxes on the 15th of July.
- Well, you would then open your cart in June and use the entire month to get customers signed up and generate revenue.
- You would then close your cart right at the end of June.
- You would use the revenue you generated to pay for products.
- You still have 15 days until the first round of boxes is due to be shipped, so there is plenty of time to order products and pack the boxes.

This is actually a very similar strategy to the one we used in BusterBox when we were getting started. We were struggling financially when we decided to launch, so we didn't have a choice but to do it. There wasn't a chance we could afford to pay for lots of products upfront. Especially when we didn't know how many we would even sell.

THE DIFFERENT TYPES OF SUBSCRIPTION BOXES

It is important to know that there are two different types of Subscription Boxes. I will break down each model below so you have a clear understanding of what they are:

1. Curation

To break it down in the simplest way possible. This is when a brand will ship out a hand-picked selection of products to their customers on a regular basis. Customers love this type of subscription as it allows them to discover new and exciting products. Your goal with this subscription is to wow your customers with every single delivery.

This is the model that we have implemented in BusterBox. We will source a selection of healthy treats and fun toys each month. This saves the customer the hassle of going to the pet shop and buying toys and treats there.

If you choose this model, it is a good idea to create new themes each month and source your products around those themes. This keeps things new and interesting for your customers and helps to reduce your churn rate. If the customer thinks you are just putting a bunch of random products in a box without any thought, they will get bored of your subscription very quickly and hence cancel.

Here are some example themes from BusterBox:

- **Under the sea**
- **Farmyard**
- **Zombies**
- **Theme park**
- **Party**

Each of these will include dog toys and packaging related to that theme. E.g. The zombie theme included zombie dog toys, and the insert was designed to fit a horror theme.

The curation model is extremely popular, and you will see this type of subscription box across a huge number of different niches.

2. Replenishment

The replenishment model allows your customers the chance to automate the purchase of a necessity. A great example of this would be razors. Dollar Shave Club figured this out and scaled their business to millions of subscribers. Some other examples would be dog food, cat food, cat litter, vitamins or nappies.

The model can work exceptionally well as customers know their essentials will be delivered to them in the exact quantity they need without having to think about it. We launched a dog food subscription in BusterBox a number of years ago, and our customers absolutely loved the convenience of it. They no longer had to go to the pet shop and carry heavy bags of dog food back to their house. When they signed up for our service, they got the exact amount of healthy dog food shipped to their door when they were about to run out.

The churn rate of a replenishment subscription is usually low than a curation subscription. This is because the replenishment subscription is essential, and the customer doesn't want to cancel because they would have to purchase the product elsewhere otherwise.

How Does The Subscription Box Business Model Work?

I will go into specific details about topics later in the book, but if you are only new to the Subscription Box industry, let me break down the concept so you have a clear understanding of how the business model works.

1. Website

You will create a high-converting website to send potential customers to. This website will be the place where visitors can sign up for your subscription box. It will be designed for one only thing, and that will be converting new subscribers.

2. Product Sourcing

You will source a selection of high-quality products each month that you can package in a nicely designed box. Your goal is to impress your customers and make every month feel like Christmas when the box arrives. If you decide to go with a replenishment subscription, you will ensure your product is high quality and make the experience so convenient for the customer that they would never consider cancelling.

3. Billing Schedule

There are many different ways you can structure your billing schedule. Obviously, a lot will depend on what kind of subscription you set up. Your setup will be completely different if you have a monthly subscription versus a bi-monthly or a quarterly one. I will explain to you what we do in Buster Box and why we do it.

Back in the early days, it was very straightforward. When a new customer signs up, they would be billed straight away, and that date would be their renewal date for the duration of their subscription.

E.g., A customer signs up on the 1st of July. Well, the next time we charge them will be on the 1st of August. Then the 1st of September and so on.

This is an easy way to set up your billing, and your customers will have no problem understanding this schedule, either. It makes a lot of sense why you would charge them on the same date every month. The main reason we went with this option was that it was the only configuration supported at the time on the platform we were using. There is nothing wrong with this setup, and I know many businesses use it, but I believe there is a better way to do it. I think it makes a lot more sense for a Subscription Box to have a set billing date each month for renewals. This is a better setup because it gives you a much better idea of what your monthly cash flow will be like.

Example:

Imagine you had 5000 subscribers who pay $30 on average each month. Well, if your renewal date was the 1st of each month, you would expect to see close to $150,000 come into your bank account when that date comes around. Once you know the exact figure, you can budget your month to ensure profitability. You can also put a process in place to reach out to subscribers whose cards failed and try to save as many of them as possible before their box is shipped (I will touch on this in more detail later in the book). Both setups can work. Still, I think this way just makes things easier for the business owner regarding forecasting, so I recommend doing something similar with your business.

4. Shipping Schedule

We used to only have one shipping date in BusterBox. All the boxes were shipped on the 15th of each month. It did not make a difference when you signed up. This was the shipping date. This proved effective for us in the early days, especially regarding stock control and cash flow. We would have a good idea of how many boxes would be going out by the 1st of the month, and we would order our stock. Then if we ended up selling out, we would reach out to our suppliers and get more stock shipped to our warehouse closer to the time.

This meant we never had much cash tied up in stock. The majority of products that arrived in our warehouse were shipped out within a few weeks' maximum, and we ran a very lean operation. (We had to, as we didn't have the luxury of having a lot of money in the bank to do it any other way) Honestly, it worked well to our advantage. So, if you are getting started and are on a tight budget, you could do a similar setup.

We eventually reached a point where we had to change this setup. Even though this approach was great for us, it wasn't ideal for customers. Depending on the date a new customer signed up, they could wait a very long time for their first box. This is not a good experience, especially in this day and age where you are being compared to amazon. We had a cut-off point in our business of the 13th of each month. If you signed up before this date, your box was shipped on the 15th of that month. If you signed up after this date, you had to wait until the 15th of the following month. That meant some customers waited for 6 weeks until they received their first box.

Predictably, this was not a great way to welcome a new customer on board, and we found that if somebody was waiting such a long time for their first box, they were much more likely to churn. So we changed our setup and started shipping the first box within a few days, and then the following boxes are shipped on the 15th of each month. This is much better for the customer and has helped us reduce some of that early churn. I would recommend you make it a priority to eventually switch to a similar schedule at some stage as well.

5. Fulfilment

You will ship your boxes out to your customers every month (or whatever the shipping schedule is). This can either be done by hiring a fulfilment centre to manage this for you or by renting your own warehouse and employing staff to help. At the very start, we used to ship boxes out of my house. Eventually, though, this got to a point where it was no longer feasible, there was too much stock getting delivered, and we couldn't move inside the house.

We then moved into a small office that had some storage. This was great, but after a year, we outgrew this space as well. We then shifted to a much bigger warehouse which had multiple floors and plenty of space. We stayed in this warehouse for several years and employed staff to pack our boxes.

Then Brexit happened, which meant we could no longer ship boxes from Ireland into the UK without going through a lot of hassle. The only solution was to move our packaging to a fulfilment centre in the UK which we still use to this day.

In my opinion, there are positives and negatives to packing your own boxes and to using a fulfilment centre. Usually, packing your own boxes will be cheaper (especially at the start), but it can also take up an enormous amount of time. Even if you hire help, you still need to manage those people. Once you start growing, you may also find yourself in a position like ours where you need to keep finding bigger locations.

Fulfilment centres are a bit more expensive, but if you find a good one, it can take away a lot of your stress and give you more time to focus on growing your business instead of worrying about packing boxes.

Both options can work it just depends on personal preference. Now that I have explained how the business model operates, let's jump straight into the steps you need to follow to build your dream Subscription Box Business.

CHAPTER 3
Picking Your Niche

I hate to break it to you, but despite what some people say, not every niche can successfully be turned into a Subscription Box or Subscription Product. Yeah, sure, you can try it, and it has been attempted with nearly every product you can possibly imagine, but unless the numbers and metrics make sense, it doesn't matter how good you think your idea is; it will fail.

In the very early days of the Subscription Box Industry, the apparent success of companies like Birchbox and Dollar Shave Club sent the hype around this business model through the roof! There was a lot of excitement around anything to do with direct-to-consumer, and investors were licking their lips at the thought of what other items or niches could be adapted into a subscription-based model.

A lot of people thought you could replicate what companies like Dollar Shave Club were doing with nearly any direct-to-consumer product and have a lot of success. I am afraid the real truth is that this isn't the case at all, and unless your subscription-based business model has a few critical components, it will be extremely difficult for it to work.

Let's break down these key components so you can ensure your business has them from the very start.

1. Potential For Low Churn

These businesses do not work well at all with high churn. If you have a high churn rate, it's nearly impossible to make the numbers work.

In case you don't know what churn means, let me explain.

This is simply the percentage of customers who cancel your subscription during any given month.

Your bare minimum churn rate with a direct-to-consumer product should be 10% or under. That is the number you should be working towards when you launch. This number wasn't pulled from thin air, and there is a very good reason why it should be 10% or under. If your churn rate is any higher, the sheer amount of customers you will need to get every month to stay where you are subscriber-wise or to grow further will be through the roof.

Here's an example:

If you have 10,000 active subscribers and your monthly churn rate is 10%, this means you are losing 1000 subscribers per month. You would need to keep finding 1000 new subscribers every month just to stay exactly where you are in your business.

Depending on your niche, this is certainly possible to do.

But imagine your churn rate was 15%. Well, in this case, if you had 10,000 subscribers, you would need to get 1500 new subscribers per month just to stay where you are. That is harder to do, and it's also a lot more expensive to maintain as you need to find an extra 500 subscribers per month. Not only is it difficult to find this sheer amount of customers every month it is also very expensive and is putting a lot of strain on your marketing department.

Now imagine your churn rate was 20% with 10,000 subscribers. Well, in that case, you now have to get 2000 new subscribers signed up every month just to stay where you are.

Now it's becoming nearly impossible to get this amount of customers signed up, and your marketing spend is eating into your profits every month. At this point, it is highly likely your business isn't sustainable anymore and doesn't make any kind of financial sense.

That's why churn is so important, and you have to be very careful when picking your niche. Pick something where the customer is likely to stay around for a long time. Do not pick something where you are keeping people for a few months on average. If you do this, you are making life much harder for yourself.

You need to be extremely strategic when picking your niche to ensure you pick something which has the potential to keep the churn low. When I originally started doing 1-on-1 private consulting, I was shocked by some of the metrics I was looking at. There were businesses that were only keeping people signed up for three months on average, and the owner was dreaming of scaling up and acquiring thousands of subs. I am afraid with a churn rate that high, it simply isn't possible to achieve this because, on average, you are burning through your entire subscriber base every three months.

Obviously, there are things you can do to help reduce your churn rate, which I will touch on later in the book. So if you have been running your box for a while and you have high churn, don't panic, as you can improve it. If you are only getting started, you should be strategic when selecting your niche so you give yourself the best chance of success with this business model.

There are many reasons why your churn can be so high, but a lot of the time, it is down to the niche. If you pick something which consumers aren't interested in receiving on a repeatable basis, you are giving yourself a mountain to climb.

2. Potential For High Margin

One of the biggest reasons why a Subscription Box fails is because the numbers never make any sense, and a poor margin is normally the driver of this. I have spoken to Subscription Box owners who charge over $30 for their box, but their gross profit is only $2 - $3 per box. I am afraid with a margin like this, it would never be possible to build any kind of sustainable business. This is because the numbers don't make sense whatsoever.

If you earned $3 per box and got 1000 people signed up, you would only earn $3000 gross profit per month. This simply isn't enough to cover costs and pay yourself a salary. As your business gets bigger, your overheads will increase, and you need to ensure you are able to pay them.

Here are some of the costs to consider

1. Customer Service
2. Salaries
3. Insurance
4. Software
5. Office / Warehouse Space
6. Marketing

Now, unless you were running a high-volume subscription business with a very cheap customer acquisition cost, a small profit margin like this would never be viable. It would not make a difference how many subscribers you got signed up. You would just keep burning money over and over again.

The advice I give to new subscription box entrepreneurs is to aim for a 50% gross margin with your box. If you manage to achieve this, the numbers make a lot more sense, and you can build a very profitable business on a strong foundation.

Here's an example:

If the average price of your box was $30 and your margin was 50%, then you would earn $15 gross profit on each box. This is much better and will give you the foundation to build a sustainable business.

If you had 1000 subscribers, you would earn $15,000 gross profit per month.

If you had 2000 subscribers, you would earn $30,000 gross profit per month.

If you had 3000 subscribers, you would earn $45,000 gross profit per month.

This is why I encourage new entrepreneurs to do their research and only go into a niche where they can earn a gross margin of at least 50%. If they manage to do this, they are giving themselves a big advantage, and the entire business will be much easier to scale.

Obviously, there will be exceptions where you can get away with a lower margin. It's usually if you charge a high price for your box or the customer acquisition cost is cheap, a lower margin can work.

It is very important that you don't bury your head in the sand and ignore what I just covered in this section though.

You want your business to be a massive success with the potential to change your life when you get 1000 subscribers signed up. One of the most frustrating and saddest things that can happen is when somebody reaches this level, but the margin is so bad they are still burning money and can't even pay themselves.

Do not let that happen!

When you reach 1000 subscribers, make sure you are getting paid well, and your business is very healthy. This is an amazing achievement to reach this level, so you want to ensure you are getting rewarded for all of your hard work at this point. To ensure this happens, you need to earn a strong margin on each box.

When you are getting started, it may not be possible to reach a 50% margin straight away, and that is completely fine. Normally you have to reach a certain number of subscribers where economies of scale kick in, and you make more profit.

You need to do the research though and find out what that level is.

When we were starting BusterBox, we spoke to all of our suppliers and couriers at the start and asked them what level we would have to be at to hit certain price breaks. This was very helpful as it gave us goals to aim for where we would be earning more profit. I recommend you do the exact same thing.

3. A Big Enough Market To Sustain Growth (You Will Always Have Churn)

There is no point dreaming of building a $10-million-dollar Subscription Box business if the niche you pick is tiny and there aren't enough customers to buy your product. It is possible to build a successful business with a small, passionate niche, but you just need to ensure your goals are in line with reality.

The fact of the matter is no matter how good you are, you will always have churn in your business.

You need to be aware of this when you pick your niche. Otherwise, you can find yourself in a position where your target market is so small you end up burning through the entire market, and there is no room to grow.

When we were starting BusterBox, the first thing we did was check how many dogs were in the UK. We could see at that time, there were over 10 million dogs. We understood that not everybody who owned a dog would be our ideal customer, but we knew there were enough dogs to support a very healthy business.

I find it crazy that people jump into starting a business without doing the most basic research about how big their market could potentially be. I do understand that for some niches, it is harder to find the information, but a lot of the time, it will be there if you spend a bit of time looking.

We simply Googled how many dogs were in the UK, and we found a few reputable sites that contained the information that we needed. This will probably be the same for you, and if it isn't the same and the information is a bit harder to find, you should still spend time looking into it. This is the most basic market research and is very important to your success.

4. Does Your Target Market Have Purchasing Power?

I will give you a very powerful piece of advice: Do not try and sell to the unsellable, AKA Broke people. If you pick a niche where the target market is people who can't afford or see the value in your product, you have picked the wrong niche. Trying to sell to people that don't have enough money to purchase your Subscription Box repeatably will end in tears. It will be hard to get people signed up, you will end up with high churn, and it will be impossible to get the numbers to make sense.

In an ideal world, your niche will be full of people with disposable income who see a lot of value in what you're doing. You don't want it to be the case when your customers see their credit card bill. They enter into a state of panic and cancel their subscription. If this is the path you are going down, it is going to be very hard to make this business model work for you.

You want the situation to be completely different. You want your customers to be really excited when their box arrives, and they don't even flinch when the renewal goes through on their card. They love what you do, and they don't mind paying for it each month.

Back when we were doing the initial market research for BusterBox, this was something we knew we had to get right. There was no point in setting up a business if the customers didn't have purchasing power or weren't willing to pay what we needed to charge each month to make the business viable.

We simply conducted some more basic research where we went to Google, and after a few searches, we could see what dog owners were spending on their pets each month. We then worked out a ballpark figure of what we were planning to charge. We could then see that our business model was viable and we would be able to make a healthy profit on each box sold.

I recommend you do the exact same thing before you start your business. Make sure you do some basic research to try and figure out what your potential customers are spending on similar products which will be in your box each month. If you see that they are already spending enough to sustain your potential business, you are probably onto a winner. This is because they are already willing to pay what you charge, and it will then simply be a matter of turning them into your customers and making sure they buy those products from you.

A lot of this information will be publicly available if you search on Google. In the rare case where you can't find it, you will have to dig a bit deeper. This may involve going to places where your potential customers hang out. ETC. Forums, Reddit, Facebook groups, etc. and getting permission to survey them to find out this information.

5. How Difficult Is It To Advertise To Your Target Market?

This is something that a lot of people don't consider when they decide to select their niche. If you pick something where it is tough to advertise to your ideal customer, it is much harder to succeed. If you can't recruit customers in a cost-efficient way using the usual marketing channels, things can be very difficult.

You should spend some time thinking about this and doing a bit of research before proceeding.

I would do the following:

- **Check the targeting options in Facebook ads**

Do you think it will be possible to reach your ideal customer by running ads on Facebook? Facebook isn't the be-all and end-all, but it normally is one of the top-performing channels for most Subscription Boxes.

- **Check monthly search volume on Google**

If you create a Google ads account (which is free), you can use one of their tools called keyword planner to check the search volume around your product. When you click on that, select the option for search volume, and then you will have the opportunity to enter some keywords which are related to your box.

This tool is very handy because it will show you how many people are searching for these keywords. If it's the case, there is plenty of demand, then Google ads could potentially work well for recruiting customers to your box.

E.g., if a lot of people are searching for cat toys every month, it is highly likely there is demand for a cat toy subscription.

- **Research influencers in the space**

Influencer marketing can work very well for Subscription Boxes. You should do some research and see if there are any influencers who are in your space and would be passionate about your box. This can be a very cost-effective way of getting people signed up.

- **Check forums / Facebook groups**

Are there any forums or Facebook groups where you could potentially advertise your box? Some of these places allow businesses to pay to advertise relevant products that the members may like. If there are plenty of communities where you can do this, it can be a great avenue for advertising your box.

- **Check other marketing channels**

Is it possible to reach your target through other channels that I didn't mention? E.g. TikTok, Pinterest, Snap, Direct Mail, Radio, Events, ETC. Depending on the niche you pick, some of these channels can be very powerful.

The point I am trying to make is unless you are in a niche where you can recruit customers in a cost-effective manner that makes sense financially, you don't have much of a business. I have come across some amazing entrepreneurs, but they have put themselves at a massive disadvantage by picking something where it is like pulling teeth to get customers signed up.

Before you jump into anything, have a serious think and make sure you have a plan on how to recruit customers for that box. Obviously, you will develop your skills as time goes on, and you will get better at marketing, but it is still important to have a basic plan for how you will grow from the start.

When my two business partners and I decided we were going to set up a Subscription Box business, we had a couple of ideas on what niche we wanted to get involved in. The first option was some kind of fitness box, and obviously, the second option was a dog subscription box.

Let me explain to you how both ideas managed to tick all the boxes mentioned above.

1. Both Had The Potential For Low Churn

You could focus on a sub-niche of the fitness market and recruit some extremely passionate customers. You could then bring them on a journey each month with your box and help them reach their fitness goals and assist them in its maintenance.

Example:

- Yoga for women over 30
- Weight lifting for Vegans
- Specific types of Diets.

This had the potential for low churn because there was a real reason why these people were signing up for your box. They were passionate about achieving their goal, and your box could help them with that. Once you were providing a lot of value, the potential for low churn was high.

We also knew we could get the churn to a low level with a dog subscription box business. Dog lovers were going to the pet shop anyway on a monthly basis and buying this stuff. So we knew if we kept the box fun, gave good value and provided world-class service, we would be onto a winner.

2. Both Had The Potential For A High Margin

A fitness box has the potential for a high margin because, depending on what sub-niche you pick, you can charge a high amount for it, and you can also boost your margin further by adding some digital elements to the experience. E.g. online training classes, online membership, online diets. These digital elements have little to no hard cost and can make a massive difference to your overall margin.

When we looked at the dog subscription box, we knew that once we hit a certain size, we would then be able to cut out all the middlemen and get our own products produced directly in china. This would improve our margin massively. We could also see the potential for adding things like tough toys, which would also really help the margin. This made the dog subscription box idea very appealing to us.

3. Both Markets Were Big Enough To Sustain Growth

We knew that both markets were big enough for us to build a very healthy business in either niche. We did some research and saw the UK pet market was worth £5.9bn, and there were over 10 million dogs and growing. When we looked into the fitness market, we could see that it was worth over £3 billion and still growing.

Both opportunities looked massive to us. We knew Subscription Boxes were still a new enough concept, but in time people would get used to them, and they could really disrupt either industry.

4. Both Markets Had Purchasing Power

We knew that people had no problem spending money on themselves when it came to their health and fitness. We are coming into a time in society where people are taking more and more pride in their appearance and their health. We also knew that passionate dog owners had no problem taking out their wallets when it came to looking after their dogs. This meant that either niche would be a good option for building a sustainable business.

5. You Could Advertise Easily In Both Markets

It wasn't going to be that difficult to advertise in either niche. You could use a wide variety of different marketing channels to reach customers. Facebook ads looked like they had big potential. There was plenty of search activity on Google, and we also knew that influencer marketing had the potential to work for both as well.

This put us in a difficult position where we didn't know what to pick. The fitness idea seemed very promising, but there was one thing holding me back. I didn't really know much about the industry, and I barely even went to the gym. I could hardly be an advocate for health and fitness when I spent more time relaxing in the jacuzzi than lifting weights.

We decided to go with the dog idea in the end. We were all dog lovers, and I had had a dog since I was five years of age. I went to the pet shop regularly looking for toys and treats and actually had a genuine interest in that. My two business partners also thought we would have more fun with the dog box. We could come up with some pretty crazy marketing, and it would be very rewarding to bring so much joy into the lives of so many dogs.

So the big question is, what should you pick for your niche?

I have given you my thought process on what makes a good subscription box niche. But it is also crucial that you pick something which you have a genuine interest in. I was never a big believer that all you need is a passion for building a business. I actually believe that is a harmful way of going about things.

People take that quote, and they run with it and don't think logically about anything else. There are some other factors that are important, and if you don't have them, then you will fail. It doesn't matter how much passion you have if the numbers don't make any sense or if there is no market willing to pay for your product.

I think the key is finding something which you are interested in and also ticking all the boxes I mentioned above. I think you do have to have some passion for what you do. Otherwise, you may end up quitting when things get tough, and trust me, when it comes to business, things can get tough very quickly. So it's all about having a bit of passion for what you do but mixing that with real practicality so you can build something which is sustainable.

I have spent the last few years completely submerged in this business model, and I have come across many different boxes. Some have become massive successes, and others have completely failed. A lot of this is down to the niche the business owner originally selected.

Here are some of the niches which can work very well with the Subscription Box Business Model:

1. Animal / Pet Box

This is a niche I know very well, considering I own a Dog Subscription Box company. A Dog Subscription Box isn't the only type of pet box you can do, though. There are loads of opportunities in this space.

People have emotional connections with all different types of pets, and you can build your Subscription Box company on that.

Examples:

- Hamster Box
- Cat Box
- Fish Box
- Bird Box
- Bunny Box
- Dog Food Subscription
- Cat Litter Subscription
- Specific Dog Breed – EG Pug Subscription

2. Alcohol

I am a massive fan of this kind of Subscription. I think it can be very effective as people nowadays love to try a wide variety of drinks. You also have the opportunity to build a very profitable back-end into your business with an Alcohol Subscription Box. This is because there are lots of opportunities for upsells and cross-sells.

You can boost your customer lifetime value significantly by selling other drinks to your customers through a stand-alone online store.

Examples:

- Beer Club
- Whisky Club
- Wine Club
- Gin Club
- Rum Club

3. Art And Crafts For Kids

I think this is one of the best niches you can pick for a Subscription Box. The reason why I think it works so well is it has two key elements:

a) Genuine excitement in your marketing - You can create genuine excitement in your marketing videos a lot easier when filming with kids. Once kids like the product, this is very easy to achieve. This makes a big difference to the performance of your ads as they will grab a lot of attention.

b) The potential for low churn - Parents don't mind paying for a monthly Subscription if the kid is getting something out of it and it's educational. This can lead to very low churn.

If you mix effective marketing with low churn, you get a highly profitable business.

4. Beauty

The Beauty niche has a lot of competition as some of the biggest players in the industry have built gigantic businesses. That doesn't mean you can't have your own success, though. One of the best ways of succeeding in beauty is by niching down further and appealing to a segment of passionate customers.

Examples:

- Mascara Subscription
- Skin Care Subscription
- Make-Up Subscription
- Organic Beauty Subscription
- Bath and Beauty Box
- Lipstick Subscription
- Lash Subscription
- Nail Art
- Perfume
- Earing Subscription

5. Beef Jerky

People absolutely love Beef Jerky, and the unit economics of this product can work very well for a Subscription Service. I think the best way to do this is with a Jerky of the month club. Every month you can discover a new kind of Jerky.

Then the customer has the opportunity to repurchase more of the Jerky they like from your online store. This is a clever way to increase the lifetime value of each customer.

6. Tea / Coffee

A Tea or Coffee subscription can work very well. This is another Subscription product where the unit economics can make a lot of sense. This is very competitive, but you can still have success once you find a way to stand out and differentiate yourself.

Examples:

- World Coffee Club – Try different Coffee from all around the world
- World Tea Club – Try different Tea from all around the world
- Artisan Coffee Cub
- Coffee and Book Club
- Have a cause built into your Coffee / Tea Subscription

7. Keto

The Ketogenic diet is a very low-carb, high-fat diet that shares many similarities with the Atkins diet. It involves drastically reducing carbohydrate intake and replacing it with fat. This reduction in carbs puts your body into a metabolic state called Ketosis.

This diet has gained a lot of popularity in the last few years, and it would work well for a Subscription Box business. You could sell digital products such as diet plans or mini-courses to help cover the ad spend. Then your physical box could contain snacks, ingredients, supplements and sauces to help people stick to the diet and make it a success.

8. Monthly Book Clubs

This is a great niche to get involved in, as there are so many passionate readers out there. A lot of people like to actually read with a physical book now as well instead of digital. If you do decide to set up a monthly book club, it can be helpful to niche down further and build a community around it.

I would never just call it a monthly book club where the customer will get any random book. I would just pick one kind of book and build the business around that.

Examples:

- Romance Novels
- Science Fiction Novels
- Horror Novels
- Crime and Thriller
- Kids Book Club

Then, once you pick the kind of books your business will be built around, you can start to include additional products each month that suit the theme of your box.

9. Socks

This is another Subscription that can work very well. Let's face it, men and women need a regular supply of socks for obvious reasons. The unit economics of this product also makes a lot of sense from a Subscription Standpoint.

If you do decide to go down this route, I would lean heavily into humour and try and make the socks as colourful and funny as possible so you stand out in the marketplace.

10. Travel Box

I really like the idea of this Subscription Box. Why not create a Monthly Subscription that will transport your customers to a different part of the world each month?

Every month the theme of your box could be focused on a different country. This would be a fascinating box for those people who love to travel.

You could also have a stand-alone E-commerce Store where customers could visit to repurchase some of their favourite products from different countries.

11. Fishing

This is a hobby that a lot of people are incredibly passionate about, and that is exactly the kind of market you want your Subscription Box to be in. You could offer a monthly box of fishing lures, accessories and all kinds of products that these customers would find valuable.

You could also add some digital products into the mix and offer training and tips to help people improve their fishing skills. I think this would work very well for a Subscription Box, and you could also have the benefit of an online store that would sell more expensive fishing products.

12. Hiking / Adventure

A Hiking / Adventure box has the potential to do very well. This niche is full of passionate people who do not mind spending money on equipment or accessories for their hikes. This box could target anyone who loves exploring the wilderness and the mountains.

The products could include outdoor gear, apparel, food, and emergency tools. If you decide to go down this path, I would 100% add an educational aspect to your offering. You could share tips in a digital format and also build a very strong community around this. People who go on adventures love to share pictures and recommend places to each other. This would work very well in a Facebook group.

13. Comic Book Subscription

This market is full of collectors who are highly passionate about their hobbies. With the right kind of marketing mixed with exceptional service, it won't take long to build up a Subscriber Base. You could ask people who their favourite characters are and then tailor their monthly box around that, or it could be a mystery box with a collection of new and vintage comics.

Comic book collectors love talking about their passion, so this is another Subscription where you should be aiming to build a strong community behind your product.

14. Meal Delivery Subscription

This kind of Subscription is becoming increasingly popular with busy professionals who no longer have time to shop or prepare food. There is a lot of competition in this niche, but you can still have a successful business if you understand how to market your product correctly.

There are a couple of different directions you can go with this one:

- The exact ingredients are delivered along with recipes (So the customer can still cook their own food and save the trip to the shop)

- A weekly supply of meals that are prepared and just have to be placed in the Microwave.

Both approaches can work.

15. Baking Kit

This can be an excellent Subscription Box for parents who want to do an activity with their kids. Your monthly box could contain measured dry ingredients plus step-by-step baking directions. This is something that could be a lot of fun and teach kids a new skill in the process.

I imagine you could build a great community around a business like this, where people would share tips and pictures of the cakes they have baked.

CHAPTER 4
The Perfect Prelaunch

Once you have decided on what niche you are going to pursue, you should be ready to run a simple test to verify the demand. A common mistake new Subscription Box owners make is they don't bother doing this, and they end up jumping in head first.

This can leave you in a situation where you waste a lot of time and money going down a rabbit hole that won't ever bring you the results you desire. I see this all the time, somebody picks a niche, and then they start ordering large quarantines of cardboard boxes and products upfront. Before they know it, they have run up a large bill, and they end up under a lot of pressure.

Then if the demand for the subscription box isn't there, the situation turns from bad to worse pretty quickly.

This is not the correct approach you should take when you are planning to set up a subscription box business. The correct way to do it is to run the following test to establish what the demand is like first.

Let me explain how to do the test below:

- **Take professional pictures of a mock–up box**

You should put together a mock-up image of the type of box you are planning on launching. You don't need to waste time and money on a branded box just yet. You can simply go on amazon and purchase a few boxes in the style you are considering and use one of those for this test. You should be able to order low quantities, and they will be delivered in a few days.

You then need to source the same type of products that you would consider using if you did go ahead and launch this box. When I tell people to do this, they normally get bogged down and start trying to set up merchant accounts with suppliers to get a few products for pictures.

Let me explain to you what we did with BusterBox when we were running this test. We went to the local pet shop, and we purchased some products that would be suitable for this test. We knew we would be using similar products if we went ahead and launched the business, so this would work fine for us. You should do the exact same. For the majority of niches, you can go to Amazon and purchase everything to fill a mock-up box in less than an hour. 9 times out of 10 companies will be fine with you doing this, but if there are any doubts, reach out to the company who made the product and make sure this is ok.

Then you are going to want to order some coloured tissue paper or put together a sample leaflet so the mock-up box looks appealing. The whole point of this is you want the mock-up box to look as close to your finished product as possible without wasting a lot of time and money in the process.

Once you have done that and you are satisfied, you then need to take some professional pictures of the box. This is the point that many people mess up when it comes to this test. They end up taking some very poor-quality pictures with their phone in poor lighting, and the box looks so bad that nobody is interested in buying it.

Getting a few professional pictures done isn't expensive at all, and for the purpose of this test, it is a necessity. If you Google photographers in your area, you will be able to hire one for a couple of hours.

If you don't have the budget to hire a professional photographer, I recommend purchasing a lightbox from amazon. This will make a massive difference to the quality of your photos.

- **Put together a landing page**

The next step in the process is putting together a landing page that you can use to capture emails. There are many different ways you can do this. You can use one of the Subscription Box platforms like Subbly, or you can use a funnel platform like ClickFunnels or Kartra, or if you want the cheapest option, you can put something together using WordPress pretty easily.

On the landing page, you will need to do the following:

- Write a compelling headline
- Upload a professional picture of your box
- Come up with a really good offer so potential customers will leave their email and join your waitlist
- Let people know you will be launching soon

Once you have created this landing page, you then want to send traffic to it to see what the demand is. It really does not make a difference where you get the traffic from once you ensure you are targeting people whom you think would be a good fit to sign up for your box.

Here are a few ways to generate traffic:

1. Facebook Ads

You can use Facebook ads to quickly start sending traffic to your landing page. The good thing about this is you can generate traffic immediately with this approach. Facebook still has the largest selection of targeting options, so it's likely your target customer can be reached.

2. Facebook Groups

You should search Facebook and join as many groups as possible which are relevant to your niche. You can then speak to the moderators of the group and work out a deal to advertise your new box.

3. Influencers

You can pay influencers for a shout-out to promote your new box. The key here is to do the research and make sure you find the right influencers who are targeting the same niche as your box.

4. TikTok Ads

This can work very well because, like Facebook ads, you can reach your ideal customer and start generating traffic immediately.

TikTok now has over a billion users, so it is very likely your ideal customer can be found on this platform.

5. Reddit Ads

Depending on what niche you pick, Reddit can work very well for this. This is because there are so many subreddits where passionate people meet up to discuss various topics. If your niche has a good following here, this can be powerful.

6. Google Ads

If your type of box is getting a decent amount of search volume on Google, then this can be a great way to generate traffic quickly. This is intent-based traffic, so if you can use it to collect leads, they can end up being extremely high quality. Intent-based traffic is very different compared to the traffic you generate from platforms such as Facebook. As with intent-based traffic, those people are actively searching for terms related to your box. This is why the lead quality can be so high.

There are many different ways to generate traffic, collect leads and get subscribers, and I will touch on them in more detail later in the book. For now, though, you just need to figure out if the idea you have come up with has potential. If you follow the process I described above and you start collecting a solid stream of leads, then it is likely people are going to be interested in purchasing your subscription box in the future.

If it's the case, you are sending relevant traffic to your landing page, and barely anybody is entering their email address. Well, it is a terrible sign. It usually means there is no demand for what you are planning. This isn't nice when something like this happens, but it is much better to learn this information as soon as possible instead of wasting a lot of time and money on something which won't work out in the end.

Make sure you run a fair test with a good amount of traffic when doing this. E.g. at least 500 – 1000 visitors minimum before assuming anything. I have witnessed people do this test, and after ten visitors and no emails collected, they have decided the business won't work. This is not enough data to make any solid conclusion.

Also, if your landing page doesn't convert, don't give up on your idea straight away. Tweak your offer and your messaging and give it a chance. If it's the case that no matter what you do, though, there is little to no interest in your box, I wouldn't proceed with it. I would change to a different subscription box idea.

Landing Page Offer

When you are running this test, it is imperative that you have a very irresistible offer that you will give in exchange for a visitor's email address. I will go into detail on marketing and offers later in the book, but I need to mention it here as well, as it is so important to this process.

If you don't come up with a very appealing offer, it is very likely you will struggle to collect leads. You have to put yourself in the customers' shoes. They have never heard of your company before, and they are getting bombarded with marketing messages hundreds of times a day.

So it's a heightened probability that they have become numb to ads at this point and definitely don't have any intention of giving their email address to a company they never heard of before. The way you solve this problem is by coming up with a really good offer. When your offer is really irresistible, it cuts through all the noise, makes your customers pay attention, and then takes action.

Here are some example offers that I have witnessed work very well for this:

- **Founding members discount**

This is one of the most powerful offers when running this experiment. You can position it that anybody who enters their email address will be given the opportunity to sign up for a lifetime founding members discount. This makes your offer more exclusive and can also help reduce your churn rate, as people won't want to cancel because if they decide to sign back up, it will be at a higher price.

- **15% lifetime discount for founding members**

This also helps your early subscribers build up a positive connection with your company as they feel like they are in an exclusive founder's club. I have witnessed this kind of offer work time and time again.

- **Exclusive free gift**

Another offer that can work very well when testing this concept is to give founding members who sign up a free gift with their first box. We do this kind of offer all the time in BusterBox, and it works great. If you are going down this path, make sure the free gift is something that would actually get your target customer excited. If you do this correctly, it can make a massive impact on the number of people who sign up.

Example: In BusterBox, one of our most successful offers was a free home camera when somebody signed up for six or twelve months. We positioned the offer that customers could use the camera to keep an eye on their dogs and communicate with them while they were at work. This worked very well as so many people were returning to the office after covid and felt guilty leaving their dogs behind.

If you are making a free gift offer in pre-launch, you would simply have a picture of the gift on your landing page along with a brief paragraph explaining when you are launching and that the first hundred people would get this free gift with their first box so leave your email, so you don't miss out.

- **Deep Discount**

A lot of people will tell you that you shouldn't discount your product because you will devalue it. This can be true in certain cases, but discounts can work great as an offer. The secret to doing it correctly is to ensure you know your numbers and that you only discount the first box on a six or twelve-month subscription. This way, customers need to commit for a long period of time if they want that discount. That is a great way to repeal all the freebie hunters and discount chasers who would otherwise sign up for one month, take the discount and then cancel their subscription straight away. A discount can work extremely well when doing this, as it's a great incentive to get somebody to hand over their email address.

This would be positioned similarly to the free gift offer on the landing page. You would simply say the first hundred people or whatever number you choose is getting a discount on the first box, so leave your email here, so you don't miss out.

Proceeding with Prelaunch

Once you have verified your idea has demand, then you can proceed with your pre-launch. The whole point of a pre-launch is to create hype and ensure that when you launch, there is a bunch of people ready to sign up straight away. This is the best way to launch a Subscription Box business because it gives you a solid platform to build from and will give you a spike in revenue from day one, which can be used to purchase products.

I explained above how to test your new idea. This is the same strategy that you should proceed with to continue to collect leads for your pre-launch. It is vital to collect as many leads as possible to ensure your pre-launch goes well and you get off to a good start in your business.

They say that the average pre-launch list converts at 10%. I don't personally believe this. It can convert much higher if you build a solid connection with your leads and create genuine

excitement around your launch. Or it can convert a lot lower if you end up making a mess of everything.

When we launched BusterBox back in 2016, we made a big mess of our pre-launch, and because of this, we ended up only getting twelve people signed up the first month. I still look back at this time with regret and know it could have went a lot better.

The reason why our pre-launch never went to plan was down to a couple of different factors. The first big problem was we kept changing the date we were meant to be launching on. This is because work was getting done on the website, which took longer than expected. This created confusion with our list, and once this happens, things never go well.

The main reason it flopped, though, was that we didn't warm up the list correctly. We simply never sent out enough emails, and we never created enough excitement in the build-up to our launch. This is actually the biggest reason most launches fail. The business owner does the hard bit and generates the leads but then makes a mess of the easy bit by not warming them up.

You have to understand the average person has a million different things going on at once, and just because they handed over their email address at one point doesn't mean you are always going to be top of mind to them. If you aren't emailing them enough or sending out boring emails, they will forget about you or unsubscribe from your list pretty quickly.

It's your job as a business owner to ensure neither of these things happens. You need to get your list so excited and engaged about your box that when you finally launch, they are ready to take out their credit card and purchase from you straight away. The correct way to do that is to warm up your list, which I am going to explain how to do below.

Email Automation

You need to ensure you are emailing your new leads regularly to keep them warm. The easiest way to do this is to set up automation using email software like Active Campaign or Mailchimp. You should be emailing your list at least once a week at a minimum when you originally collected their email. Then as launch day approaches, you should start emailing them more regularly. When you reach the point that you are four weeks away from launch, you can start emailing them three times a week. When you are two weeks away from launch, you should be emailing them four times a week. Then for the first week after you launch, you should be emailing the list every day to get as many sales as possible.

You can share sneak peeks, ask for feedback, tell your potential customers where your brand is going, share testimonials, share helpful information and create urgency around your launch. The whole point of these emails is to build up hype and anticipation so that when you launch, you have a bunch of hungry buyers ready to sign up.

Here are some email ideas:

1. Welcome email

You welcome new leads to your list. You confirm with them the date you are

going to be launching. You give them a brief rundown of your company, and you invite them to follow your social media pages.

2. Sneak Peek email

You give your leads a brief breakdown of the progress you are making. Then show them some sneak peeks of a few products and possibly your box design. Remind them of the launch date and the limited offer they will get if they sign up. You can send many different variations of this email showing off different products in the run-up to launch.

3. Feedback email

This is probably my favourite type of email to send out. I like it so much because you learn valuable information which you can use to improve your product. Your customers also love it because it makes them feel like they are a part of a company that actually listens to what they want.

You create a survey using something like SurveyMonkey and then email it out to your list, asking for feedback about your box. You explain to your customers that you want to serve them to the highest standard possible and to do that, you would like to ask them what kind of products they would like in future boxes. You can then use this information to improve the customer experience going forward. You would also remind them in the email of your launch day.

4. A reminder email

As your launch day approaches, you can send out a simple reminder email. You should tell everyone that a lot of people have joined the waitlist, and if they want to ensure they don't miss out, they should be ready to buy as soon as you go live. You can also reveal another sneak peek of your box here to build up anticipation further.

5. Launch email

When launch day comes around, you should be ready to email your list and remind them it's now time to buy. Make sure your email contains your unbelievable offer and make it clear that there are a lot of people on the list, and you can't guarantee they will get the offer unless they sign up now.

Then after you launch, you should continue to email the list and follow up regularly to ensure you get as many people signed up as possible. You usually get the most people signed up the first day, but then plenty more come through in the following days when you follow up.

If you follow the exact strategy which I just discussed above, you will have a very successful pre-launch, and you will end up with a solid number of subscribers to build from. The test concept is vital, and you need to do it because, honestly, the last thing anybody wants to do is waste a lot of time and money working on something nobody is interested in. Once you have verified the demand, though, you are good to go, and you should work to get as many leads as possible and then use a basic email sequence, as I discussed above, to warm them up.

It goes without saying that if you want to be successful in this industry, you have to be very active on social media. You should create your pages at the beginning of your pre-launch. When we were getting started with BusterBox, we created Facebook, Instagram, and Twitter pages immediately and started putting out dog-related content.

You should do the exact same thing with your business. You should spend some time coming up with some niche-related content that will resonate with your target audience. This will give you credibility when people look up your brand during the pre-launch phase. It is also a great way to engage directly with potential customers. We now have over 80,000 followers across all of social media, and this has helped us massively with growth.

If the pre-launch doesn't go well, don't panic because all is not lost. Our pre-launch went terribly in BusterBox, and we only managed to get twelve people signed up. That didn't stop us from going on and selling millions of euro's worth of subscription boxes. You can do the same. If the pre-launch flops, analyze it and see where you went wrong, and learn from it. Then dust yourself down and continue building your business. Remember, with strong marketing skills, you will still be able to go on and build a highly successful subscription box.

Once you have completed your pre-launch, the real fun begins. You now have paying customers, so that means you need to get ready to ship your first box.

CHAPTER 5
Sourcing Products

If this is your first time learning about a Subscription Box Business model, you may be wondering where you will actually source your products from. The answer to this question really depends on what niche you choose. When we decided to start BusterBox, we spent a considerable amount of time putting together a list of all the pet suppliers we wanted to work with. We were passionate dog owners, but we did not know a lot about the dog industry or where to source products from.

To solve this problem, we created an excel file to track suppliers and then spent time on Google searching for them. After a few days of research, we had a list of all the main dog toys' and treats' suppliers in Ireland and the U.K.

We then put together an email and reached out to all of them one by one. We introduced ourselves in the email, explained what we were planning to do and then told them we would love to work with them going forward. If we never got a response to the initial email, we would follow up with another email, call their office directly, or we would reach out to one of their sales reps via LinkedIn.

It took a bit of time, but eventually, we had a database of suppliers whom we would be able to work with going forward. Obviously, there are specific places you can go for products like Etsy, Alibaba or AliExpress, but for the majority of niches, the process that I explained above is the correct way to source products.

I wish I could list a few websites that would carry all the different types of products at prices that make sense but unfortunately, it doesn't work like that. For instance, if you decided to set up a craft beer subscription. Then you would have to spend some time reaching out to all the craft breweries and sourcing your products that way. Likewise, if you decided to create a cat food subscription, you would have to spend time reaching out to all the cat food manufacturers and source your supply of cat food that way.

When I am consulting for new subscription box owners, one of their biggest concerns is getting the best price possible from a supplier once they have identified them. This is only natural as everybody wants to ensure they make the most margin possible from their box. I am afraid when you are only getting started, though, and you don't have the volume to support your claims of how successful you will be, it's hard to convince the majority of suppliers or manufacturers to give you the biggest price break possible.

The correct way to go about it is to build up credibility with a supplier and show them over time that you are a good company to deal with. Pay them on time and back up your claims of growth with an increase in volume when you order from them. If you do this and build a good relationship with your suppliers, you will find that it is a lot easier to ask for price breaks.

This is the exact approach we took. We kept speaking to our suppliers and negotiating as our business grew and kept asking them about price breaks. We knew that when we reached a certain level, things would drop in price. So this gave us a goal; to aim for where we would be earning more money.

You can also do things like: If a supplier has a big product range that you would be interested in using, you can say to them that you are willing to use a certain number of their products over the next 12 months if they can give you a better deal.

E.g., You are dealing with a dog toy supplier. They have 4 dog toys you would be interested in using in your box. So you give them a guarantee that over the next 12 months, you will use all 4 toys. You will just space them out and put them in the box every 3 months, so your customers aren't seeing too much of the same brand.

You make it clear to them, though, you will only use them 4 times if they give you a good price on the products. This is usually a good negotiation tactic to help increase your margin.

When we first started working with some of our suppliers, nobody took us seriously. They were charging us the maximum price on all the stock that we ordered. Over time though, we managed to build great relationships and all the prices dropped considerably.

This is the exact same approach to take when it comes to asking for credit. If you are only a new company and you have no credit history, the majority of suppliers will not do it if you start asking for credit straight away. It takes time to build up trust, credit history and a good reputation, but once you do that, you will be able to ask for credit and get it.

One of the best things about the Subscription Box model is the fact that you have a very good idea of how many boxes will be getting shipped out in advance. This makes it a lot easier to forecast numbers when ordering stock.

One of the biggest problems with straight eCommerce is if you don't get your forecasting right, you can end up with a lot of stock building up in your warehouse. This can end up eating into your profits and causing chaos to your cash flow. With a subscription box business, it can be completely different.

Imagine you decided that on the 15th of every month, you were going to ship out all of your boxes. Well, in that case, all of your stock could arrive by the first of the month and the majority of it can be shipped out by the 15th and turned into cash.

This is one of the main reasons why we were able to grow BusterBox with not much money at the start. We were very strict with this approach and we did everything in our power to get out as much stock as possible within two weeks. Obviously, there will be months when you don't manage to clear everything but that is fine. The benefit of this model is, you can use your existing stock on new customers' boxes the following month. Once your customers are getting quality boxes, it does not make a difference if it is stuff from the previous month. They will not know this and they won't mind either once the box is to a high standard.

As your business grows, you will want to get to the point where everything in your box starts becoming your own brand. There are a few different reasons why you want to do this and it's very important to the long-term success of your business.

The first reason why it is very important is that once you start manufacturing your own products and going directly to the source, you can earn more margin on your box. This is because you cut out all the middlemen who are earning profit from you. The more people who touch your products before they reach your box, the more margin you lose. This became clear to us after a few months.

We were working with suppliers who were sourcing products from companies who originally sourced their product from factories in China. This meant 3 different companies were getting paid for the product plus all the shipping expenses before we made any money from it.

These days, things are very different for us because a lot of our dog toys are our own brand and they are sourced directly from China. This allows us to make a lot more margin on our boxes and means the company is a lot more profitable.

When you are getting started, though, it probably won't be possible to achieve this. This is because it can be challenging to go directly to China. There are normally minimum order quantities that you have to hit to make it worthwhile, plus it can cause havoc to your cash flow. This is because you need to place orders 3 – 6 months in advance. Normally it is only worthwhile going down this path after you build your business to a certain level so you have the cash flow to do it. Or you raise money through investors at the start so you have the cash in the bank to make it happen.

The other reason why having your own brand products is very important is because it can raise the perceived value of your box to a great extent. If all of your products are your own brand, then customers can't individually price each product and feel like they could have saved money by buying things through amazon or a different retailer. This isn't a big problem, but occasionally, you will have customers who will find your products cheaper in other places and will email in to complain about this. It can be very annoying when this happens because you have no influence over what other retailers charge or what kind of deals they have worked out for those products in the background.

A way to avoid this is to have everything under your own brand so you can control the price. You can then sell some of the products you put in your box on your company's stand-alone e-commerce site. When you do this, make sure to raise the price of the products so when customers take a look, it increases the perceived value and they know they got a good deal because it worked out cheaper to get the products through your subscription box than your e-Commerce site.

This can go a long way to increase your monthly retention rate while also opening up another revenue stream for your company. Also, if you are looking to sell your company one day. It will be a lot more valuable and you will get a bigger exit if you have your own range of products compared to sticking other companies' stuff in your box.

When you are getting started, it is perfectly fine to work with local suppliers and put other brands into your box. Depending on your niche, some of your customers will actually really like this. Getting to the level required to fill your box with your own brand products should eventually be the goal for the majority of niches. However, it takes time and effort but it normally pays off for most Subscription Boxes.

CHAPTER 6
Pricing Your Box For Success

When it comes to deciding on the price of your subscription box, there are two things you need to get right.

- **The box needs to be good value for money**

If your customers think your box is a rip-off and isn't good value for money, it will be hard to get them to sign up. Even if you do get them signed up, you will have a high churn rate as they will quickly come to the realization that it isn't worth it.

- **You need to earn a decent profit from each box**

You need to ensure that you price your box in a way that you can actually earn a good profit from every sale. If you price it too low, you will struggle to make your business a success and it won't be sustainable. So both of these factors need to be considered when you are starting your business. If you manage to get both of these things right, you will be able to build a healthy business that your customers love.

When we started BusterBox, originally, we priced our boxes way too low. We completely underestimated our overheads and what our customer acquisition cost was likely to be. This resulted in us creating a lot of self-inflicted problems in the business. The reality of this situation really became apparent when we went full-time and moved into our first office.

For the first three months, we weren't earning any salary and we were just living off our savings. Things were getting tight, but thankfully by the end of the fourth month, we were able to get paid for the first time. We took a very small salary which worked out at €1000 each for a month's work. This was well under minimum wage because we were working seven days a week, twelve hours a day minimum, but I didn't care. I was never so happy to get paid in my life.

At that point, it felt like we had turned a corner. We were working full-time in our own business and we had our own office space. We started getting paid and the business was growing month after month. Within a few months, though, things started unravelling for us again. It was the end of October and we were due to get paid. When we checked the bank account, we realised there was barely any money and we still had bills to pay.

We ended up getting paid €300 each which had to last us six weeks. I can tell you now that they were not a good six weeks. This was very frustrating because, on the outside, it looked like business was going well. We were doing over €30,000 per month in sales and had really gotten a tight grip on our customer acquisition, but the reality was far different and we were really struggling cash flow-wise.

A few weeks later, I was introduced to a brilliant business consultant. We chatted on the phone and he agreed to come out to our office to help us put some plans in place around scaling up. The day he arrived, there was an article about us in the newspaper so we were on top of the world. This changed very quickly as when he took a look at our numbers, he told us bluntly what we were doing didn't make any business sense.

We were living in a dreamland if we thought this business was going anywhere with our current margins. We had all of our cogs and overheads listed on a whiteboard and he could see what profit we were making on each of our subscriptions. Our 12-month subscription had a gross margin of 22% and across all of our plans, we had an average margin of just over 30%. When you looked deeply into the numbers and actually worked out where we were heading, it didn't make pretty reading.

I told the consultant we were on track to getting our MRR to €43,000 before the end of the year which would give us a company doing over half a million euros a year in sales. He painted a picture of what the situation would look like when we reached that goal. Even at €500,000 per year in sales, we wouldn't be able to hire any help, we would be working round the clock and we would be earning just above minimum wage.

That didn't seem like a success story for a company generating that much revenue. It actually seemed like a complete nightmare. When we started BusterBox, if somebody told me we would get to over €43,000 per month in sales, I would have thought I would have been extremely comfortable and earning a great salary. I certainly didn't expect it would result in working seven days a week and getting paid less than I was when I worked part-time in a supermarket.

The whole problem stemmed from the metrics and the margin in the business. I will cover subscription metrics later in the book and explain how important they are but for now, I will just cover the margin. An average margin of just over 30% on a relatively low ticket subscription is simply not enough in most cases. As a typical rule of thumb, you want your gross margin to be 50% or higher.

Now obviously, there are certain exceptions. If you are in a niche with lower competition which can mean lower customer acquisition costs, it may be fine to have a lower margin. Also if you sell a higher-priced subscription box, you may be able to get away with a lower gross margin because the margin is worked from a higher sales price. It really depends on your business and there is no 'one size fits all' answer to this, but for the majority of these businesses, the aim should be 50% or higher to ensure you are comfortable and you are building something which is actually sustainable.

Now when you are getting started, it may not be possible to achieve a 50% margin straight away and that is perfectly normal. Usually, you need to reach a certain number of subscribers before you start getting price breaks with suppliers, couriers, and packaging companies. You should do your research thoroughly and make sure you know at what level your margin will be increasing. Then, you should work as hard as possible to ensure you get there as quickly as possible.

Thankfully, we had our wake-up call in BusterBox many years ago and we now have a business that has a margin of over 50%. It was not easy to reach this goal but we eventually got there through a mixture of increasing prices, getting bigger, and cutting out a lot of middlemen who were supplying our products and going directly to the source.

It's also very important to note that when you are working towards your 50% margin, you need to ensure your customers are getting value for money. There is no point in raising your prices to hit the 50% margin if there are high chances that your customers might start to think that your service is a rip-off because the contents of the box are worth nothing close to the price you charge.

Each BusterBox contains two high-quality toys and three bags of healthy treats wrapped up in a fun theme. It usually works out better value than if you went to the shop and purchased similar products individually. This makes the customers more loyal because they know the product is great value for money and the dogs love it.

You may need to work on your product offering if you can't get close to that 50% margin. You should look into the number of products you are offering along with the type of products you are offering to see if it is possible to switch them up. This way, you can make more money and the customer gets more value.

Example: You send out a monthly beauty box. Your margin is very weak and when you look into your numbers, you realise it is near to impossible to make your business model sustainable.

Each box you send out contains four sample products and one full-sized product. You charge $20 on average for each box and your gross margin is 20%.

You decide to switch the concept up and change what you are offering in the box. Instead of four sample products and one full-sized product, you change it to six full-sized products.

Instead of charging $20, you change the price to $60 per month, and instead of making a 20% gross margin, you now earn a 50% gross margin.

You should do a similar exercise if your business doesn't make any sense. Don't kill the concept; just switch up your offering so you make a better margin. One of the biggest mistakes you can make with your subscription box is pricing it too low. If you fall into this trap, you will end up in a position where it is basically impossible to make your company a success.

I have witnessed this happen to so many different subscription box companies and it is very sad when it occurs. It doesn't make a difference how smart you are or how hard you work. You will not be able to outwork or outsmart bad maths. Eventually, it will catch up with you and put you out of business. You may have a wonderful subscription box that your customers love. You may have the best website and best team in the world. I hate to break it to you but none of that makes any difference at all if you can't generate a profit for your box.

Let me break down for you what usually happens when you price your box too low.

1. Can't afford to advertise

You quickly find yourself in a position where it isn't possible to advertise across different channels. You start writing them off one by one.

"Oh, Facebook used to be great but it's too expensive for me now."

"Google seems promising but the CAC is too high and the numbers don't make sense."

"TikTok is amazing but I can't use it as it's too expensive."

"Influencer marketing is a waste of time for me because it's too expensive."

The bottom line is: if you are in a business which can't afford to advertise then you won't be able to get customers and if you don't have customers then you don't even have a business to begin with. Customer acquisition costs are increasing all the time and you need to put yourself in a situation where you can afford to keep advertising. You can help with this by pricing your box correctly so you have a strong margin.

2. Not able to hire help

If you price your box too low, you will not be able to afford to hire help to support the growth of your company. This turns your business into a self-inflicted prison where you end up burning out eventually. Yeah sure, it's fine at the start for a new founder to do many different roles but this isn't something which should go on forever. As your company continues to grow, you will need to build out a team so you can focus on doing the more important tasks, which actually moves the needle. These businesses are great but they do need manpower to get anywhere. Things such as customer service, marketing, design work, web development, and fulfilment are just some of the areas where you may need to hire staff to help.

One of the most common reasons I see people struggling with this business model is because they try to do everything themselves. They end up with a couple of hundred subscribers and can't afford to build out a team to take the business to the next level.

Then when you look into their numbers, you realise that the margins are so tight it doesn't make a difference how big they get; they will always struggle to pay additional staff.

3. Can't afford to pay yourself a decent salary

When you first dreamed of setting up your subscription box business, you pictured a reality where you earned more money than in your job, you had more freedom and you could take care of your family. If you leave your margins too tight, your business will never be able to help you achieve this.

When you are starting out, it is perfectly normal to get paid little or nothing from your business. What isn't normal though is running your subscription box business for five years and getting paid less than minimum wage or nothing at all. It is fine in the early days to be living on the bare minimum and scraping by but it isn't fine as you get older and can't afford to buy a house or have a good standard of living.

You need to ensure when you reach a goal like 1000 subscribers, it is a massive success and you are getting paid well. It is difficult to get to a goal like this so when you do achieve it, the sacrifice and hard work needs to be worth it and you should be rewarded. One of the saddest things to see is somebody running their business for years and they manage to grow their revenue to seven figures and over 1000 subscribers and they still can't even get paid a decent wage. Do not fall into this trap. Look deeply into your numbers and make sure you are on the right path early on.

4. Can't afford to pay general business expenses

Things such as insurance, warehouse space, software etc. are all required. If you have a poor margin, you will be struggling to pay for some of this stuff. This simply can't happen. All businesses have overheads and general expenses that need to be covered. If you can't cover them, you can end up in a lot of trouble.

How to ensure you don't have a bad margin or price your box wrong?

As you can tell, pricing your box wrong and having a bad margin isn't good at all. Now that I have made you aware of what can happen, let me explain how you can avoid this trap from the start. Firstly, you should do regular price testing to determine the maximum amount you can charge without completely destroying the volume of subscribers you get signed up.

This is how most Subscription Box companies determine their prices:

The company is about to launch and the founder decides to do some price research to understand what they can charge. So they spend some time googling a few competitors to understand what they are charging. Then, they decide to price their box the same or slightly cheaper so "customers will sign up because you are cheaper." At last, they launch their business without any further price testing and stick to these prices for good.

Please ensure you do not do this. This is a terrible way to conduct price testing.

If you do this, you are 100% leaving money on the table. This is because basing your pricing on what competitors charge is actually extremely dangerous.

This is why...

1. You don't know if they have some kind of competitive advantage that isn't clear.

2. They probably didn't do the correct research themselves when deciding on their own pricing.

Number 2 is extremely common and the by-product of this is, you end up with a number of companies in the same niche where all of them copied each other's pricing. Now every single one of them are charging too little and struggling.

This is the correct way to do price testing:

You need to do some market research and figure out roughly what you think you can charge. You will then go with that as your initial pricing to start. You then need to ensure you have Google Analytics set up on your website and you are tracking your conversion rate and your CPA (Cost per acquisition). You will then run traffic to your website for a week and you will track your conversion rate and your cost to acquire a customer. Then, you increase your price for new customers by 10-15% and see what happens.

Has your cost to acquire a customer gone up? (If it has only gone up slightly, the increase may still be worth it with the higher customer lifetime value you are now getting). Has your conversion rate dipped? Are your sales falling off a cliff? Has it made absolutely no impact whatsoever and you are now earning more money on each sub? (Highly likely when you are just raising it slightly at the start).

You then repeat the process the following week and increase your prices by 10-15% again and look at the data and see what happens. You will then keep doing this every single week until you finally hit that price barrier where sales completely fall off a cliff and it is no longer worth it to charge a higher price. You will then know 100% what is the maximum you can charge for your Subscription Box and you can revert to that price and stick to it.

My guess is, you probably have some assumptions about what people are willing to pay and you may be close, but you will probably still leave money on the table without doing this test. I highly recommend you do this because when you start scaling up, even a couple of dollars can make an enormous difference to how profitable your business is. Something else which you should bear in mind is market conditions change all the time. So you shouldn't settle on your existing prices for good.

We have found in our own business the price people are willing to pay now compared to what they were willing to pay a few years ago is completely different. This is probably down to the increased cost of living. However, this means you should be willing to do price testing regularly to ensure you are staying on top of things and maximizing how much you can earn from each box.

A great way to improve your margin and increase retention is to offer multiple subscription terms with price breaks for customers if they commit to a longer subscription. We have three subscription terms in BusterBox. When somebody is about to join, they have the option of selecting a 1-month, a 6-month, or a 12-month subscription. The 12-month is the cheapest because the customer is committing for a longer period of time, while the rolling 1 month is the most expensive because the customer can cancel any time they want.

This is how the 3 subscriptions are currently priced in the UK market.

- 12 Month - £21.99 per month.
- 6 Month - £23.99 per month.
- 1 Month - £30.99 per month.

We purposely make the 1-month subscription much more expensive because we want to push customers to sign up for our 12 and 6-month plans as we want them to commit for a longer period of time.

This is something which is called decoy pricing.

I learned about this many years ago and I found it fascinating. The best example I can think of is Starbucks. Next time you are queuing up for your coffee, take a minute to understand why they do what they do with their cup sizes. They are laid out and priced in a way which influences consumers to spend more which benefits their company.

They have 3 options when it comes to selecting your cup size.

- Tall 8 oz - €2.50
- Grande 12 oz - €3.50
- Venti 16z oz - €.5.00

The majority of people would probably be okay with the Tall option when ordering their coffee and it wouldn't seem worth it to pay more for the Grande option. Starbucks realised this so they added the more expensive Venti option as a decoy to push more people towards the Grande instead. The majority of people do not need the Venti option but it has suddenly made the Grande option a lot more appealing. Now the price jump between Tall and Grande doesn't seem that much, so you are more likely to select the Grande option.

Another example of this is McDonald's.

If you decided to purchase the individual items from a Big Mac meal on their own, they would work out a lot more expensive than if you just purchased the meal. McDonald's does this on purpose to sway consumers into spending more money when they visit the restaurant.

How many times have you gone to McDonald's for a snack and ended up purchasing an entire meal? I have done this many times. I have walked in not that hungry with the intention of purchasing something small like a chicken sandwich. When I look at the menu though, I realise it would be much better value to purchase the entire meal and that's what I normally end up doing.

This tactic is done on purpose by McDonald's and it is very smart.

We introduced Decoy pricing into BusterBox, where our 1-month option is the decoy. We don't really want people going for this as the churn is much higher and the lifetime value is lower. So we price it much more expensive than the other plan terms and we also don't include any offers with the first box. This works extremely well because the majority of people now go for the 6 or 12-month options. It's a complete no-brainer for the consumer.

Why would they sign up for a much more expensive subscription with no offer on the first box when they can commit for longer and get an offer and, at the same time, save some money along the way? A very small percentage of people still do go for the 1-month option and because it is much more expensive, it helps to increase the average revenue per user across all of our subscriptions.

We also included an upsell in our sign-up flow which makes a big difference to our margin and helps to increase the average revenue per user even further. If you take a look at our website, you will see the customer has an option to upgrade their subscription and receive an extra premium toy each month for £6.99 extra. Depending on the month, we have 20 – 30% of consumers selecting this option when they sign up. Because shipping and all other costs are already covered, this is very lucrative for us. We can source dog toys for a very good price so we make a very healthy profit margin when somebody selects this option.

I would highly recommend you do something similar with your Subscription Box business. You will always have a percentage of customers who are willing to pay a bit more. If you don't give them the option to do this, you are leaving a lot of money on the table again. It doesn't even need to be complicated. Just give people the option to pay a bit extra to receive an extra product each month. I guarantee that a good percentage of people will start going for it and it will help your margin out a lot.

When you are calculating your margin, you should work it out on the average revenue per user. At the start, you can work it out on a per subscription basis but long term it makes a lot more sense to do it by the average revenue per user. This is because it gives you the full picture of what your average margin is across all of your subscription plans.

I will cover metrics in more detail further into the book but for now, let me summarise what your average revenue per user is and how it is calculated.

Your average revenue per user will paint a clear picture of how much a single customer is worth to your business.

ARPU= Monthly Recurring Revenue (MRR) / Total Active Users.

So, imagine a Basketball Subscription Box business was doing $100k per month and you had 2000 subscribers.

$100k / 2000 = 50

In this case, the average revenue per user would be $50.

Now, I do not recommend trying to work out what your ARPU is manually or any metric for that matter. It is important that you have software which can do this for you, so you know everything is 100% accurate and can be monitored in real-time. We use a piece of software called ChartMogul, which is very good. I would also recommend looking at ProfitWell, Baremetrics, or Sublytics. All of them will give you the information you need; it just depends on which one is compatible with your platform.

When you are certain you know what your correct ARPU is, you can then work out your gross margin.

When working out your gross margin, you need to include all costs of goods sold. E.g., every cost which needs to be covered when fulfilling a box:

- All products
- All packaging
- All processing fees
- Shipping
- Fulfilment
- Any other cost to fulfil the box

A common mistake new Subscription Box owners make is, they don't include payment processing fees when doing this calculation. You need to ensure you include them as they can add up over time and you want to paint an accurate picture.

Now we already worked out that the BasketBall Subscription Box we mentioned above has an average revenue per user of $50. Well now imagine the average COGS are $25.

Well, in this case, the owner of this company would be earning $25 profit on each box sold.

This is pretty decent and means the gross margin across the subscription is 50%

$50 (ARPU) - $25 (COGS) = $25 (Profit)

$25 (profit) / $50 (ARPU) x 100 = 50% Gross Profit.

That is a good profit margin for a Subscription Box business and with 1000 subscribers, this company would be earning a gross profit of $25,000 per month. This would mean the owner of this fictional company is on track to building a very healthy and profitable business that can actually scale.

This is what you want to aim for when creating your Subscription Box business. If you have a business like the one I just mentioned above, everything will be much easier for you and you will get the rewards you deserve for taking the risk of setting up your own business.

CHAPTER 7
Creating A Website That Converts

Now there are many different options to choose from when it comes to selecting what platform to build your website on. We use a platform called Subbly which I would highly recommend. There are also a number of other good subscription platforms like Bold, Shopify, Cratejoy, or Recharge. You could also build an entire custom solution if you had the money to hire developers. Personally, I don't recommend this for 99% of new subscription boxes, though, because it can turn out to be expensive and a lot of hassle and the out-of-the-box solutions are good enough to start with.

A lot of the platforms have similar features, and at the end of the day, it usually comes down to preference on what one you choose. We went with Subbly because their customer service is fantastic, and there are a number of key features the platform has which allows us to run our business smoothly. When you choose your platform, the next step would be building your website. A common problem for new subscription box owners is they don't have the skills to build a website that will actually convert.

The minimum conversion rate you should be aiming to hit for a mid to lower-priced subscription box is 2%. The reason why you need to be hitting a 2% conversion rate is that otherwise, it will be extremely expensive to grow, and converting visitors to subscribers will feel like pulling teeth. Advertising costs are increasing all the time, and you need to be making the most of your traffic. If your website is converting less than 2%, it will be very hard to make your operation profitable.

Now, when you are getting started, you normally aren't thinking about any of this. All you are interested in is building your website to the best of your ability so you can start getting subscribers. The realisation that you need to improve your conversion rate normally occurs after you have been running for a while and you have been struggling to get traction. I am going to save you a lot of time and effort because I am going to explain exactly how your website should be designed for maximum conversions.

The layout which I am going to share has produced a conversion rate of up to 7% for BusterBox on some offers. A lot of my private clients have also used it over the years, and when done correctly, it has improved the conversion rate for all of those businesses. Something to bear in mind, though, is that you can apply this layout, but if your design is poor or it looks confusing, you will struggle to get traction. So make sure everything is done to a high standard. That includes getting professional pictures of your box. Whether you like it or not, when you start advertising, you will be competing with some big competitors, and customers will go with them if your website looks amateur and makes customers feel worried about putting their card details in.

Subscription Box website layout for maximum conversions

- **Header**

The first thing a potential customer is going to see when they visit your website is your header. If they don't understand what you offer, pretty much immediately, they will leave your website, and you will end up with a high bounce rate. You only have one chance to make a good first impression, so this part is extremely important.

The test I get people to think about is. If you brought somebody in from out on the street and sat them down on your office chair and loaded up your website, would they be able to tell you what you do within a couple of seconds? If the answer is no, it means your message isn't clear, and there is some confusion. The aim of the game is to keep things as simple as possible. Something very important to understand is.

"Confused customers do nothing."

If any part of your sales process is in any way confusing, it will be an uphill battle to get people signed up, so you want to avoid that. For the majority of Subscription Boxes, the header should contain a professional picture of your box with one of your target customers holding it or sitting beside it, looking very happy with the experience. The box should be open, and it should be packed with some of your best products. You should never lie in your marketing materials, but you should make sure you put a picture of one of your best-ever boxes as your header image. This will get potential customers very excited and give them a good idea about what they should expect.

You should also have a headline that explains exactly what you do in the simplest way possible while also selling the product. In BusterBox, we used the headline "A monthly box of dog goodies" I don't think we could have made it more obvious than that.

Here are some more examples from some of the biggest subscription e-commerce companies:

- **Dollar Shave Club** – The $9 Razor Starter Set
- **Birch Box** – Meet Your best friend in beauty
- **Fab Fit Fun** – Join the shopping membership over 1 million members love.
- **Blue Apron** – The meal kit that puts quality first.
- **Breo Box** – A box full of fun, curated, new gadgets delivered to your door every quarter.

You will notice that each company uses a headline that leaves nothing to chance. From looking at a combination of their header image and their headline, you will understand exactly what they offer after looking at their header for a couple of seconds max. You should aim to do the exact same in your business. Do not try to be too clever, and do not try to allude to anything. Just make everything as obvious as you possibly can.

Here's another example headline I came up with for a Kids' Craft Box.

A monthly craft box bursting with fun activities to inspire creativity in children.

This summarises exactly what this business does in one quick glance; nothing is left to chance. Make sure you do the exact same when writing your headline.

Also, touching on my previous point about the professional photos. It is absolutely essential that you do this. You can get away with a lot of normal photos from your phone when creating your ads, but this is not a good idea for your website. You need to portray your box in the best way possible. You also want to build trust with potential customers, so they know you are a legitimist business. The worse way to destroy credibility is by having a poor-quality website full of low-quality images. You are expecting people to take out their credit cards and commit to a monthly subscription. This can be a hard sell unless you have everything perfect.

If you want to see the quality of pictures which you need, I would suggest visiting any of the following websites:

BusterBox.com

Dollarshaveclub.com

Fabfitfun.com

Glossybox.com

Or any of the other big subscription companies that have managed to achieve massive scale.

- **How it works section**

When building your website, make sure you include a 'how it works' section. This is really important for subscription boxes because what you are offering is completely different from a straight e-commerce company. With a straight ecommerce site, the sales process is very simple. If somebody buys a product, the shipping time is displayed on the checkout, and the customers know when to expect it. With a subscription box company, there are more questions that need to be answered. The simplest way to do this is with a how it works section.

We have this section broken down into three simple steps.

- **Step 1 Subscribe to BusterBox.**

Monthly dog joy is just a click away. Starting from just £21.99 / €25.99

- **Step 2 We ship your goodies.**

Your first box is shipped immediately and all remaining boxes are shipped on the 15th of each month.

- **Step 3 Your month–long dog party begins.**

Every day is playtime with BusterBox. Valued at over £40

This 3–step process breaks down in the simplest terms how our service works.

In section one, we explain the price. In section two, we explain how shipping works and when the customer should expect their box. In section three, we explain how much a typical BusterBox is worth. Now we didn't just randomly decide to include this information. The reason why it is there is that these are the main questions a customer has before they take out their credit card and sign up.

A lot of subscription boxes follow different shipping schedules and a customer is less likely to sign up if they just missed the last shipment and have to wait a long time for their first box. That is why we make our shipping schedule clear in section two. Also, one of the main reasons which stop somebody from signing up or makes them cancel is when they feel like they are not getting good value for money. When this happens, it really annoys customers, and I don't blame them either. I wouldn't be happy if I signed up for a $ 50-a-month subscription and each box was filled with junk with the typical contents worth just $15.

That's why in section three, we make it clear that our box is valued at over £40, which is a lot more expensive than the customer will pay to start a subscription. This section removes one of the biggest barriers, which kills conversions.

When you are designing the how it works section, make sure you make it as simple as possible so any potential customer can follow it without much effort. I recommend following the exact outline that I mentioned above.

- **What's Inside Section**

I find it crazy the number of people who don't bother adding a 'what's inside' section to their website. At the end of the day, you are expecting people to commit to an ongoing subscription where the contents change each month. If the customer can't get an idea of the standard of products that will be included, then it is highly unlikely they will be tempted to sign up. That is why you should have a clear 'what's inside' section on your website. This doesn't have to be complicated. Just a clear picture of one of your boxes and a brief explanation of the type of products that will be arriving on a monthly basis.

Then as time goes on, you can add another section containing pictures of previous boxes. This is a great way to showcase all of your best boxes and show potential customers that if they commit for a long time, they can expect to receive high-quality stuff every month.

- **Social Proof**

Selling any kind of Subscription product without social proof is rock hard. People will want to see proof that you are a good company with a great product before committing to a long-term subscription. That is why it is very important to add as much social proof as possible to your home page. We signed up for Trustpilot in BusterBox because this is a fantastic way of displaying social proof. Customers know that Trustpilot can't be manipulated and that whatever reviews are on the website are true.

I recommend you do the same in your business or, at a bare minimum, collect reviews from customers and display them on your website. If you are only getting started and don't have any reviews, you should give out some free boxes to friends or influencers in exchange for a real review. Then you should post that social proof on your website. Then once you start getting real customers signed up, you should email them regularly and ask for reviews and then put the best ones on your website.

This isn't always possible, but what we found is if you can get customers to send in pictures of themselves with your box, it makes a big difference to the conversion rate. When potential customers see these types of pictures, they know the social proof is legitimate, so they trust it, and they are more likely to convert.

- **A Featured In Section**

A featured in section is designed for one thing and one thing only and that is to add more social proof to your website. It would give your brand authority if you appeared on TV, Radio, or on any well-recognized media outlet. We have appeared on TV multiple times, Radio, and in all the big newspapers in Ireland, so we make sure to list them all. When you are starting out, you probably won't have anything to put here. This is perfectly normal, but over time opportunities will present themselves to your company, and you can then list them here. To get started, you should send out boxes to some blogs in your niche in exchange for a review. You can then list those blogs in the featured section. This is also a good way to build up backlinks for your website, which will help with SEO.

- **Instagram Feed**

An Instagram feed packed with pictures of your box which were posted by real customers, can make a massive difference to your conversion rate. We are very lucky in BusterBox because we are in the dog niche, and people love sharing pictures of their dogs with our boxes. So we get thousands and thousands of images that we can use. If your box is in a niche where people are less likely to share pictures, then you can incentivise them to do that. You can run a competition and tell all your customers that you will give out a free 3-month subscription in exchange for the best unboxing video or image.

This normally works really well and, when done correctly, will leave you with an influx of images and videos that you can use for your marketing materials. In my experience, it is worth it to run this competition on a regular basis, so you always have fresh material.

When I was adding an Instagram feed to the BusterBox website, I did this. I created a brand new Instagram account, and I added my favourite eight pictures that customers sent in. I then connected that feed to our website. The reason why I did it this way was that I knew these images were extremely high quality because they were already converting users through ads. So I knew if I added them to our website, they would only help boost our conversion rate. I was correct. Once we did this, the conversion rate did improve because we now had some more great social proof on the website.

Something else to bear in mind when designing your website.

A potential customer does not want to read a novel when they land on your home page. If your home page is packed with walls of text, the majority of people are simply not going to read it, and it will hurt your conversion rate. Yes, it is extremely important customers understand what is going on but trust me, too much text is actually a bad thing. If you have long paragraphs of endless text on your home page, you need to change this. The first thing you should do is take a step back and try to figure out if all of this text is necessary. If it isn't, get rid of it or try to find a way to shorten it. Keep your messaging as clear and concise as possible.

Remember, the majority of consumers don't care about your aspirations or goals. They simply care about what you can do for them.

The job of your home page is to sell your box, nothing else. If something is necessary and you are struggling to shorten it, you can use other design techniques to get the message across. E.g., diagrams and pictures.

There is a time and a place for long-form copy, but for the majority of subscription boxes, it isn't necessary, and you could find that it could be hurting conversions, especially if most of it is irrelevant to the customer.

Also, in my opinion, your subscription box website should not sell any other product at all apart from your Subscription Box. The reason behind this is if you sell loads of different products on this website, you are likely to lower the conversion rate of your box.

You don't want to do this. Your box is the thing that you need to focus on growing because, if done correctly, that is the thing with the highest customer lifetime value, and it is also the thing that will grow the monthly recurring revenue in your company. You can and should sell other products, but the place to sell them is on a completely different website. You can advertise this website separately, or it can be a place where you can send existing customers to purchase more products after they have signed up to increase their customer lifetime value further.

One of the biggest mistakes a new subscription box owner makes is to make an attempt to sell a million different things on their website at once. They think this is the right approach because if you give customers more choices, they will buy more things. I am afraid this is wrong and what is more likely to happen is the customer will get confused and buy fewer things and probably not purchase the subscription box at all. Normally when I suggest this to somebody, they get annoyed because some fake Shopify guru told them that they should list a million things on their site at once.

Some other pages you should add to your website would be the following

- **Contact us page**

I find it crazy that so many businesses don't bother adding any kind of contact us page. You need to ensure you have one. Customers can get nervous about signing up if they think your support is a joke and it won't be easy to reach you.

- **Our story**

You should also have a simple page which explains the back story of your company. You can also add your team members' bios to this section and fill potential customers in on your company's mission.

Sign Up Process

How you structure your sign-up flow is one of the biggest factors which impacts your site's conversion rate. One of the worst things you can possibly do is have a poorly designed sign-up process or nothing in place at all. If you head over to the BusterBox website, you will see the way we have structured ours. We have a quiz funnel in place, and the customer has to answer some questions about their dog before they can sign up for any subscription.

There are a couple of different reasons why we took this approach. The first reason is we want to ensure every dog gets a box suitable for their size. This is very important; otherwise, churn will be through the roof if we are shipping out unsuitable products. The other reason we do this is that we want the customer to make a number of micro-commitments before they actually sign up for the subscription. This helps the conversion rate because the customer gets more and more invested in the product as they answer more details about their dog.

Obviously, you don't want to scare them away by getting them to fill out too much information, but getting them to answer a few questions can actually increase the chances that they sign up.

I will explain the exact layout of our sign-up process now and why we do certain things.

- **Step 1 — Dog's name**

We want as much information about the dog as possible. This way, we can improve our marketing efforts by doing very personal emails using that information. When a customer sign-up, we can also improve our relationship with them by using their dog's name in communication.

- **Step 2 — Dog's size**

This is an obvious one. We have to ask about the dog's size, so they get the correct products. Nobody will be happy if the toys are too big or too small for their dog.

- **Step 3 — Dog's breed and birth month**

We use this information to deliver suitable products each month. We also use the dog's birthday to potentially sell other birthday gifts to the owner when that date is about to come up.

ep 4 — Enter your email address

..e collect the customer's email addresses here so we can market to them if they don't complete the checkout process.

- **Step 5 — Choose your plan**

  The customer can see the price of all of our different subscriptions and choose how long they want to sign up.

- **Step 6 — Add another toy**

  The customer has the option to add another dog toy to their box with this section.

- **Step 7 — Complete checkout**

  The customer adds their shipping information and makes payment to complete the order here.

Now, as you can see, we have seven steps in our sign-up process. A lot of marketers will tell you that you want to remove as much friction as possible. This can be true for some products, but in my experience, when it comes to a subscription box, it can actually improve the conversion rate by adding some friction. I would highly recommend finding a way to implement some kind of quiz funnel into your business, no matter what the niche is. Obviously, don't just ask a load of questions for the sake of it. You should take a step back, though, and try to figure out what data you should be collecting from your customers to improve their experience, lower your churn and make you more money. In my experience, it doesn't matter what niche your box is in.

There are always questions you should be asking to improve your customer's experience.

Now, something key happens between **step 4** and **step 5,** which I need to highlight. You will notice the email collection point is placed right before the customer can see the subscription terms or our prices. We have done that for a very tactical reason. When you place the email collection point there, you collect a very high amount of email addresses from your traffic.

We place it in step 4 because, by the time the customer has reached this point, they have already completed a few steps and made some micro commitments along the way. This means they are more likely to enter their email address when they reach step 4. If we placed the email collection point as step 1 in the quiz funnel, it would actually drive people away because they know little about our intentions, and they would probably think we are going to spam them. We also purposely placed the email collection point before the customer could see our prices or our subscription terms. We did this again for another tactical reason. By the time the customer gets to step 4, they are very invested in the signup process after supplying some information about their dog. They are also curious enough at that point to supply their email address to find out what our prices are and what subscription terms we offer.

I have to say this works extremely well. We managed to collect a lot of leads every single day. This is really critical, especially in today's day and age when traffic costs are getting more and more expensive. You have to make the most out of the traffic you get, and this really helps us to maximize it. Suppose a customer doesn't sign up straight away from one of our ads. That is fine. There is a good chance we have collected their email address, and we can then follow up with them that way. This is giving ourselves multiple opportunities to try and sell to them in the future.

We are also collecting assets for BusterBox every single day with this sign-up flow. Every time we collect a new email address, that is an asset for us. This makes our business more valuable if we ever decide to sell it in the future. Most potential buyers will find a gigantic email list extremely attractive because they know once those contacts are maintained and kept engaged, they will be able to sell more products to them, which will increase their lifetime value even further

We do this ourselves and sell other dog products from our online store to people on this list. We particularly see a big increase in revenue in the run-up to Christmas when we sell a lot of hampers and one-time gifts to the list. Think about how much more money you would make and the subscribers you would get if you were collecting thousands of new leads every single month. It would be a complete game changer for your business, and that is why you need to implement what I just covered.

Other website conversion tips

1. You need to understand why people are leaving your site

If you are confident that you are sending high-quality traffic to your site, but your conversion rate is low, you need to make sure you understand what is driving your visitors away without purchasing. To do this, make sure you have Google analytics set up so you can track exactly what is happening with your traffic. If there is a particular page on your website with a high exit rate, this means this page is driving people off your website.

Let me give you an example.

Imagine you have a 'what's inside' page where you show some examples of previous boxes, and you notice this is the page where a lot of people are leaving the site. It is likely there is something on this page that is driving people away. You should take a step back and figure out what the problem is with this page. If all the pictures are poor quality and it is making the products look bad, this could be a reason. If this is the case, it is an easy fix. You just need better pictures of your box on the page to entice people to sign up.

Here's another example

If loads of people are leaving on the checkout page, it could be down to your pricing being wrong or charging shipping and not making the customer aware of this earlier in the signup process. Did you know not including free shipping is one of the biggest conversion killers? Sometimes it isn't always possible to do this, but you should try your best to make it work.

Anyway, these are just some examples of what can stop visitors from signing up. The point I am trying to make is there may be a page with a very high exit rate that is causing you problems. It is your job to figure out what's happening. If this is the case, find the problem and fix it.

TIP: You can use a program called Hotjar to measure each customer journey on your website and really analyse in detail what is going on.

2. Getting the basics right

- **Optimised for mobile.**

Around 80% of your traffic will be coming from mobile devices. (This is going to increase as the years go by) So if your site isn't optimised for mobile, you are completely killing your conversion rate. I am talking about the layout, types of pictures, and overall design. It all has to work perfectly with mobile. Suppose you are struggling to make your website mobile friendly. Then I highly recommend hiring a web designer to help you.

- **Site speed.**

If the load speed on your site is slow, you will drive your bounce rate up and kill your conversion rate. This isn't 1994, people expect your website to load quickly, and if it doesn't, they won't have any patience at all. They will simply leave your website. It should load up in a couple of seconds max, and if it doesn't, you need to find out what is slowing it down and fix it.

- **Overall design.**

If you don't have any design skills at all and the finished site looks amateur, you need to hire somebody to help you. As I mentioned earlier in the book, I learned this the hard way. I am awful when it comes to design. I tried to design our website at the start, and it took up a lot of time, and the finished product was shocking looking. If we went ahead with that design, I highly doubt we would be in business today, as we wouldn't have gotten off the ground.

You may be satisfied with your work due to the amount of effort it took, but if the site looks amateur, it will not convert well.

This could be sizing issues, placement of images and text, confusing sign-up flow, and overall presentation.

You should compare your website to the top subscription box website or other top websites in your niche. That is what your customers are comparing you to.

Honestly, in the grand scheme of things, it is not that expensive to hire somebody to design a professional website. If you are serious about your business and you want to turn it into your full-time income, it is not a big deal to get professional help.

The analogy I would use would be if you were opening a retail store, you would ensure your presentation is good and your shop is laid out in a way where you get the maximin amount of revenue from each customer that walks in your door. If your shop had stuff all over the floor, it was badly designed and had a really confusing process at the till, it wouldn't last long and you would go out of business. This is the same when it comes to your website. Now I am not saying it is bad to design your own website. If you have the skills and can make it look good and convert, then go for it. All I am saying is if it is something you are struggling with, it would be better to get some outside help to make sure it is done correctly.

CHAPTER 8
Marketing Your Subscription Box

One of the biggest factors which separate a highly successful subscription box from the one that flops is marketing ability. The barriers of entry when it comes to setting up these types of businesses are generally pretty low. I find it funny when people get very defensive about their subscription box idea and don't want to reveal it to anyone. Honestly, ideas really mean little because it's not that difficult to source products in any niche and ship them out in a box each month. There is generally very little intellectual property you can claim and protect when starting one of these. The real money and success are in the execution of the business plan and the ability to acquire customers.

If five different people all set up a subscription box in the same niche at the exact same time, the results of all of those companies would be very different. It is likely three of them would end up going out of business. One of them would get a few hundred subscribers, and the last one would build a highly successful company. Take my own company's niche, for instance. There are a lot of different dog boxes in the UK and around the world. Very few of them have managed to generate millions in sales, though. This is mainly down to marketing and the lack of ability to acquire enough customers.

That is why this chapter is going to be so important, and it's going to help ensure your business becomes a massive success. I am going to show you exactly how to grow a subscription box business. You need to make a commitment to yourself, though, that you are going to take marketing very seriously, and you are going to go all out to become an expert at acquiring customers. If you don't take control of your marketing, I guarantee that your Subscription Box Business will fail.

One of the saddest things to happen to a business owner is they become an advertising victim. This happens when they don't bother to develop their marketing skills, and they end up trying to outsource their marketing to some fly-by-night agency that doesn't have a clue on how to acquire customers repeatedly and profitably. Listen, there is plenty of good marketing agencies, and there is nothing wrong with hiring one at a certain point, but your founding team does need to develop some kind of marketing ability. Otherwise, the agency you hire can end up running rings around you. Also, when getting started, a lot of the time, it isn't financially viable to hire anybody until you reach a certain number of subscribers and you are spending a certain amount on advertising each month.

Don't worry, though, because I will teach you everything you need to know about marketing, so you can send your subscriber numbers through the roof. When we were getting started with BusterBox, we had no marketing ability whatsoever. We ended up getting twelve people signed up in the first month. Then another twenty-four people signed up over the next couple of months. We were making a bit of progress, but it felt like we were crawling, and I knew unless we got better at acquiring customers, we would never reach the level we needed to.

For the first three months, we were throwing stuff at the wall and trying to figure out what would stick. Our entire marketing strategy was based on hope. We were hoping people would sign up, and we had no reliable way of actually making that happen.

I have learned over the years that hope is the worst marketing strategy you can have.

If your whole marketing strategy is based on posting pictures on social media and hoping somebody comes across them. Then hoping they head over to your website and hoping they sign up. I am afraid you will end up in big trouble.

You need to take control, and then you need to take action to grow your company.

Everything changed for us in BusterBox as we went into our fourth month of running the company. I came across something called direct response marketing, and because of this, our Facebook ads started getting a lot more effective. We suddenly started signing up a lot more people, and over time we got better and better at marketing until we reached the level of acquiring thousands of new customers each month. Direct response marketing completely changed the game for us. Once we started focusing on this and stopped doing everything else, things started improving, and we could see our business had a bright future.

Over five years later, we have managed to sell millions of dollars of Subscription Boxes, and direct response marketing has been the main driver of that. Now, if you don't know what direct response marketing is, don't worry. I am going to explain everything and tell you why this should be the main way most subscription boxes should advertise.

Direct Response Marketing

Direct Response Marketing is a type of marketing strategy that compels a high-quality prospect to take immediate action by opting into an advertiser's offer on the spot. E.g., You get sales and subscribers straight away. Direct response marketing can be found in nearly all forms of advertising. That includes TV, Print, Online, and Radio. It costs very little to produce and all results are measurable.

This kind of marketing does not rely on one channel. Once you familiarize yourself with these principles and master the craft, these skills can be deployed successfully across a lot of different marketing channels. Direct response marketing will work for any sized business, but in my opinion, it should be the only type of marketing small subscription box companies should use.

This is because it is designed to drive the only thing which matters sales and subscribers for your business.

There are two main marketing strategies. They are branding (mass market) and direct response. When Direct Response is done right, it will deliver a return for a small business ASAP, while branding won't.

What is branding?

Branding is what all the big companies do. It is a type of advertising which aims to remind customers about your brand as well as the products and services you sell. The idea behind it is that if you run your ads over and over again, eventually, people will remember your company. Then when they eventually decide to make a purchasing decision related to a product or service you offer, your brand will be top of their mind and they will buy from you. This is how all the biggest brands in the world market. Brands such as Apple, Coke, Mercedes, etc.

What is the benefit of branding?

I am not disputing the fact that branding is extremely effective and having a strong brand presence can be very important for your company. The thing about it is this kind of marketing is usually not a good idea for a brand-new subscription box company.

This is because:

1. **It is extremely expensive.**
2. **It takes a very long time to work.**

For branding to really work, you need a gigantic marketing budget to completely saturate all forms of advertising media. As I stated, this takes time and is very expensive. This isn't a problem for big companies. They have gigantic advertising budgets and they don't need an immediate return on their investment. It does become a big problem, though, when a small subscription box company that runs out of somebody's spare bedroom starts trying to imitate a big company's marketing campaigns. When this happens, the small subscription box company will see little return on its investment and run out of money quickly.

It's not that the small company doesn't have the ability to create fantastic ads. The problem is they don't have the marketing budget to run their ads for long enough to make them effective. Without a massive marketing budget behind your campaigns, there is a high probability of failure. When a new subscription box owner starts advertising, they don't have the luxury of sitting around burning money. We are putting our personal capital in, so we need returns straight away. That is, subscribers and sales. Everything else honestly doesn't matter.

So to summarise one more time...

The main difference between direct response and branding is:

- Branding targets everybody and its main goal is to build brand awareness. When a big company advertises like this, they do not expect the consumer to take immediate action and buy straight away.
- Direct Response targets a niche audience and uses compelling messages to get an immediate response to drive a sale ASAP.

Now, my biggest teacher when it comes to direct response marketing is somebody called Dan Kennedy. I learned everything from him. I never met him personally, but I have read a lot of his books and studied his courses. It was he who opened my eyes to what was important when it came to marketing. After you finish ook, I highly recommend reading as much of his stuff as possible. It will make a big difference to your business.

Ten Rules of Direct Response Marketing

I will now go through the ten rules of direct response. It was Dan Kennedy who came up with these rules. When I first came across them, it blew my mind (In his book No. B.S Direct Marketing), and I spent time working out how to apply them to a subscription box business.

I take no credit for coming up with these. I just restructured them for my own subscription box business. Once I started applying them, it completely changed everything for us. So I am going to share them with you here so you can apply them in your own Subscription Box business and hopefully have a lot of success.

1. There Will Always Be An Offer

Rule number 1 for a reason. In my opinion, this is the most important rule. If you are familiar with me at all, you will know I love to talk about this around the clock. It's so important and it is something that a lot of subscription box companies haven't been able to grasp. If you want your potential customers to respond IMMEDIATELY, you need an unbelievable offer that is going to urge them to take action.

You should never send out an ad to a cold audience without making them an offer. If you don't bother making an offer, here are the typical results of your campaign:

- Slow sales
- High CPA
- Advertising budget is up in smoke.

The offer isn't going to be something that financially cripples your company. It has to be something that makes sense financially for you as well as entices the customer to take action. This is where metrics come into play. Things like the CPA, Lifetime value, and churn will let you know how profitable your offers are and if they are viable for your company. The offer is so important that I am dedicating a separate chapter later in the book to everything I have learned about creating the perfect subscription box offer.

2. There Will Be A Reason To Respond Right Now

Your marketing needs to entice customers to respond ASAP. This can be achieved by adding urgency and scarcity to your irresistible offer. If your prospects understand there is a chance they will miss out by not signing up ASAP, they are more likely to take out their credit card and purchase immediately.

You need to understand that potential customers have a million different things going on in their lives, and signing up for your subscription box is probably at the bottom of the pile. Once you understand this, you will know how important it is to come up with an unbelievable offer. Is some rubbish offer giving away a 5% discount on a 6 – month subscription really going to get somebody to jump out of their chair with their credit card and sign up for your box? NOPE.

These days platforms are getting more competitive, and prospects are getting bombarded with so many different ads. This means you need something pretty special to get somebody to take notice and sign up. Your offer needs to generate a direct response. That is the whole point of this kind of marketing strategy. If you can provide value to your prospects and convince them that signing up for your subscription box will solve their problems or satisfy their current desires, then your marketing will deliver results.

3. Clear Instructions

This is pretty self-explanatory, but it is something that a lot of people struggle with. I see so many subscription box entrepreneurs writing extremely confusing ads. E.g., there is too much copy and the information is all over the place. You need to put yourself in your customer's shoes. If you saw your ad appear on your feed and you knew nothing about your company, would you really know what was going on?

Remember the two golden rules.

- **Confused consumers do nothing.**
- **Most people can follow directions.**

This means your message should be so clear that if a dog on the street saw your ad, it would know exactly what was going on, and it would know how to sign up for your box. Never try and be too clever with your copy or your ad creative. You may think it's smart, but there is a good chance if you get it wrong, you are leaving a lot of money on the table.

My golden rule when writing copy or creating ads is to keep it as simple as possible.

This also applies to emails, landing pages, or any kind of communication with potential customers. Don't try anything which has the potential of confusing them and blocking them from taking out their credit card.

4. There Will Be Tracking And Measurement

Yes, that means all marketing decisions will be based on real hard facts and data. No assumptions will be made when it comes to your marketing campaigns. We all think we know what is best for our subscription boxes, but unfortunately, a lot of the time, we are completely wrong. This means you will have tracking set up correctly on any platform you run ads from. E.g., if you are advertising on Facebook, you will have your pixel set up correctly, and you will take the time to learn what the reports mean. This may be more difficult now because of all the tracking issues created by the IOS updates, but you will still do your best to get accurate information. This may mean signing up for additional software, such as Wicked reports or Hyros, to help with tracking. Or using UTM tags with Google analytics.

Since we are in the subscription box industry, you will also take time to learn about all the different subscription box metrics which are vital to the success of your company. I will dedicate a chapter to this later in the book as it's so important.

The one thing you won't do is send out a load of ads and not bother doing any of the above. If you do this, you are likely to lose all of your money. If somehow you manage to get subscribers signed up and do not understand any subscription metrics, you won't know what you even have to do to turn a profit (You could be losing money on every customer). Ultimately, you want to know what your ROI is for every dollar which is spent on marketing. This way, you can cut the ads that aren't performing or bringing you a good LTV. Once you get in the habit of tracking data, this will become second nature and a lot easier going forward.

5. Branding As By–Product

One of the best things about Direct Response is it can lead to brand building. Whenever I discuss marketing with a new subscription box owner, they tend to think I don't place any value on brand building. This isn't true at all. As I mentioned above, brand building is actually extremely important, and a strong brand can work wonders for your company. When you are getting started, you should never pay for it, though. You should focus on the most important thing in your business when investing your own capital, and that is sales and new subscribers. This means no time or money should be wasted on getting likes or getting video views. Your main objective is sales, and that is it. Sales and new subscribers are the only things that will keep your lights on. Unfortunately, Facebook likes won't pay the bills the last time I checked.

6. There Will Be Follow–Up

Not everybody is going to convert straight away, and that is okay. To tackle this issue, you need processes in place to follow up with your leads regularly. You can follow up with your prospects in multiple ways like:

- Email marketing
- SMS Marketing
- Direct Mail
- Retargeting
- Picking up the phone and calling them

The main thing is you need to have these systems set up and ready to go. If you don't bother with them and you are just sending somebody to your landing page and then letting them fly off into the sunset, it's the marketing equivalent of flushing money down your toilet.

7. There Will Be Strong Copy

This is a skill that takes time to learn. This isn't something you are going to learn overnight on some bogus Udemy course. This will require effort. Your copy needs to be strong and clear. You should know your audience so well that you are well able to provoke their emotions and make them sign up for your subscription box without a second thought.

People buy with emotion and justify with logic. You should always be aware of that when writing copy. If you need help improving your copywriting skills, I recommend reading the book Cashvertising by Drew Eric Whitman. I read it a long time ago, and it helped me improve my skills a lot.

8. In General, It Will Look Like Mail-Order Advertising

This can be a tough one to wrap your head around, but it is 100% accurate. Back in the day, before we had fancy internet marketing, a lot of companies had to generate business by advertising in mail-order catalogues. The masters of this kind of advertising could generate millions from these types of ads. You can apply the same principles to the type of ads you are running now on social media for your subscription box. If you manage to master this kind of advertising, it can be extremely effective.

Create a swipe file of any eye–grabbing ads you see in magazines or newspapers that show a clear call to action and follow direct response principles. Then the next time you are working on an ad, flip through that file for inspiration.

9. Results Rule, Period

Real results are the only things that matter in your subscription box business. This means subscribers and sales. You need to get into your head that nobody except your customers is going to put money into your bank account. This means if your marketing is bringing in sales, it is working, and if it isn't, it needs to be scrapped. Now is also a good time to dump that fly-by-night marketing agency operating out of Ohio that has been "Running Your Ads" for the last few months. When I say "Running Your Ads," I really mean setting your money on fire and bringing in no new subscribers. Instead, they jump on conference calls and tell you how much brand awareness they have brought you through page likes, video views, and competition entries. Sorry, none of that matters. If they aren't bringing in sales and subscribers, time to get rid of them and take matters into your own hands.

10. You, Will, Be A Tough–Minded Disciplinarian And Keep Your Business On a Strict DIRECT Marketing Diet For At Least Six Months

Cut the junk and bin the rubbish. Get Obsessed with these principles and master your craft, and I promise you will transform your subscription box business. It won't be easy, but if you pull it off, It's the easiest and cheapest way to get massive amounts of new subscribers.

As I mentioned, these rules were created by Dan Kennedy, and I adapted them for Subscription Boxes. Make sure to check out his stuff, and it will help you get better at marketing. Then every time you are about to run a new marketing campaign for your Subscription Box. Remember these ten rules. If you stick to this and get good at it, you have the power to completely change your business. Trust me. It's that powerful.

Now, as mentioned above, just because I am a big advocate of direct response, it doesn't mean I don't value building your brand. Having a strong brand presence is very important, but you have to build it the correct way that isn't going to bleed you dry.

Here are three Key reasons why it is important to build your Subscription Box Brand.

1. Improves Customer Retention

Loyal customers are less likely to cancel their subscription, and they are also more likely to spend more money with your company. Retention can improve significantly when your customers feel you have a strong brand. They get naturally drawn to your company and perceive your products to be better than any of your competitors, so they don't want to cancel.

This is extremely powerful when this happens; Apple is the perfect example of this. Apple has millions of fans who queue outside their shops for all their latest releases and don't mind paying more than they would for a competitor's product.

2. Improve Word of Mouth Marketing

When you have a loyal following of fans, who identify with your brand and love your box, they are more likely to recommend you to their friends. Word-of-mouth marketing is very powerful, and when it takes effect, it can dramatically reduce your CAC.

3. Lower Price Sensitivity

I hate price sensitivity. It is one of the most frustrating things about setting up a Subscription Box. The customers were right, but It used to really annoy me when somebody would spend time searching for all of our products individually on amazon and then contact us and say they could have saved a couple of dollars if they bought them separately. After a while, I realized that customers become a lot less price-sensitive once you increase your brand presence. When you have a strong brand, people do not mind paying more.

The correct way to build your brand (without going bankrupt)

As you can see, I definitely see the value in building your brand, but there is a certain way you should do it. We have been working on this in BusterBox for years and I am going to share how you should go about it. The one thing you should never do is spend large amounts of money on brand advertising. As I explained above, if you do that, you will not grow your company, and you will eventually run out of money. Stick to direct response marketing for all of your customer recruitment, but you can work on building your brand in other ways that don't cost money.

We have over eighty thousand followers across social media, but we never paid for any of them directly. All we did was run direct response ads, and a by-product of that was a lot of people decided to start following us on social media. We post a lot of different dog content across all of our social media pages. Some of the content is related to helpful tips, other content is funny stuff, and we have a good mix. Dog owners love engaging with this, and it helps us build a strong brand presence. Even if somebody is not ready to buy from us straight away, they are engaging with our content, and when it comes time to make a purchase for their dog, we are top of mind, and they head over and sign up.

We also build our brand through our communication with our customers. We have gone out of our way to hire and train a world-class customer support team. We will honestly do anything for our customers. A large percentage of them love getting in touch with us every month just to chat about their dog in general. The support ticket may not have anything to do with our product at all. All of our staff are dog lovers so they love this and they always show a genuine interest in our customer's dogs. We go out of our way to show our customers we care during every interaction. This helps us build our brand every single day.

When your customers see that you care and they have a strong attachment to your product, they will talk about your company and start recommending you to their friends via word of mouth. You should do this exact same thing in your business. You need to embrace the opportunity to speak to every customer that reaches out. You should go out of your way to ensure every interaction you have with your customers leaves them highly impressed with how you treated and communicated with them.

We also have a unique company story. We are three childhood friends who decided to set up a business together. We all love dogs, so we decided to do a dog subscription box because we couldn't find new and exciting products for our own dogs. This story is at the forefront of our company, and people really enjoy it. So it helps to give our brand identity.

I highly recommend doing something similar with your subscription box. Make sure you have a solid story that people will remember. This will draw your customers to you and get them more invested in what you're doing. The last thing you want to be is another faceless company.

We are also looking to move away from putting other people's products in our boxes. This is a long process and something you shouldn't jump into straight away. Your long-term goal, though, should be to make this happen. When you do this correctly, it can work wonders to increase your perceived value and separate you from all competitors. In BusterBox, we do a mixture of all the things I mentioned above to make our brand stronger. It works very well for us and barely costs us anything. In my opinion, this is exactly what you should do in your own Subscription Box business, It is a slow process, but over time it will help you build a strong brand and it's better doing it this way compared to spending thousands on brand marketing and awareness campaigns and running out of money.

CHAPTER 9
Creating The Perfect Subscription Box Offer

Your ability to come up with irresistible offers and present them correctly through your marketing will play a big part in determining how successful your subscription box is. Once you understand this and you get your offer right, it will make your customer acquisition much easier, and you will be able to attract floods of new subscribers. This topic deserves its own chapter because it's the most important rule when it comes to Direct Response, and it's also one of the biggest reasons why we have managed to sell millions of dollars of Subscription Boxes in BusterBox.

When somebody joins my Subscription Box Experts program, it is usually because they need help growing their business, and they want to use my proven system to scale. The first thing which I always look at is their offer. If the offer isn't correct, it doesn't make a difference how good the other parts of the marketing are because I know it's going to be a struggle to get a consistent stream of new subscribers signed up. So because of that, we always fix the offer first. I have witnessed struggling subscription boxes turn it all around and suddenly find themselves in a situation where they are acquiring more subscribers than they ever thought possible, and that comes down to one thing. The power of an irresistible offer.

Once you get the offer right, all the other parts of your marketing will fall into place.

It does not make a difference if you are advertising on Facebook, TikTok, YouTube, Direct Mail, Radio, TV, or any other channel. If the offer isn't good enough, you will struggle to get volume, and your customer acquisition cost will probably not be sustainable. The reason why the offer is so important is that without one, it can be very difficult to get people to commit to a long-term subscription. This is because people absolutely hate the thought of signing up for another monthly bill. No matter how good your product and service are, there will always be a certain level of resistance from customers simply because it is another monthly bill. You can break down this resistance and get a lot of people signed up by making your offer so good they would feel foolish to turn it down. Then once they sign up and see how much they enjoy getting their box each month. They are unlikely to cancel, and hopefully, you will keep them as a subscriber for a long time.

Your Irresistible offer is also another way that can be used to beat all competition in your niche. Imagine four different kids' craft boxes all advertising in the same market with similar products, similar reviews, and a similar service. The one who is able to come up with the most irresistible offer is the one that is going to stand out from the rest, take off like a rocket and leave the other three companies in the dust.

as 3:1 on average. The reason why you want to hit this ratio is that you will probably run into cash flow problems otherwise as you scale up.

Now that I have made that clear, I am going to highlight four key points that you should aim to hit with any offer you create. If you manage to hit all four points, you will be able to blow up your Subscription Box rapidly.

1. Volume

The offer needs to have the potential to generate a lot of new subscribers. Once your ideal customer sees it, they shouldn't be able to resist it. If you have done everything right and your ads are going out to your ideal customer, and the sales are slow, the offer is probably wrong.

2. Three to Four Month Payback Period

The maximum number of months it will take on average to get a customer into profit will be three to four months. This is after the advertising cost and whatever else you had to fulfil for the offer. If the offer pushes the payback period out any further, it will be very difficult to scale up without a considerable amount of investment in the business. Obviously, you want to get the Payback period as low as possible so you get your marketing investment back quickly so you can be profitable and reinvest some of it back into customer acquisition. If you can get it to lower than three to four months, that is fantastic, but three to four months should be the maximum for a direct-to-consumer subscription in the majority of cases.

3. Fulfilment

You have the capability to fulfil whatever the offer is without it becoming a serious struggle for your business. If it is a discount, obviously, this is easy to fulfil as it will be automatically applied to the account, but things like free gifts, themes, and double boxes take planning, and if you don't do it right and forecast correctly, you can be left holding stock which can put a strain on your cash flow.

4. Profitability

This is critical and also pretty obvious. There is no point in running an offer and signing up thousands of customers, which will never be profitable. That's why you need to pay close attention to your numbers and follow the 3:1 LTV to CAC ratio I discussed above. A new subscription box owner can tend to get excited when they discover the power of an irresistible offer, and suddenly they start getting more new subscribers in a day than they used to in a week. This makes them bury their head in the sand when it comes to subscription metrics and financial sense. Then it all comes crashing down when they realise the offer was never profitable in the first place. Don't let this happen to you.

Offer Examples

I am now going to go through some example offers so you get some ideas of what you can test in your subscription box business.

1. Deep Discount

A deep discount can work well, but if you are going with this approach, make sure you only offer it on the longer plans (six to twelve months). If you go with the deep discount on a rolling monthly plan, it will probably be a blood bath of churn. The more aggressive you get with the discount, the higher the churn. You must also accept when you are doing a deep discount; you will attract a percentage of poor-quality customers who will not be the right fit for your box.

No matter what you do, you won't be able to keep these customers happy as they only came for the discount, and they will end up canceling quickly, or their card will fail when you attempt to charge them. This doesn't mean this offer can't be profitable, though, because after the first month, when all the discount chasers leave, the churn usually drops, and the remaining customers generate a good LTV. You just have to have the correct expectations and make sure you are monitoring your metrics and cash balance.

The only time you should consider doing a deep discount on a monthly plan is when you have your funnel set up in such a way that you can have high churn but recoup a lot of the ad spend through post-purchase upsells. The good thing about a deep discount is it is pretty straightforward to set up. You don't need to manage any extra stock or anything. You simply apply an automatic coupon code to your checkout process, and that is it. When done correctly, a deep discount can grow your business pretty quickly. This is because the majority of people love a good discount which in turn sends your sales volume through the roof.

Usually, when you run this offer, you will notice the marketing cost to acquire customers moves from ad spend to product costs. This is because the CPA decreases as the offer is so attractive, but you can end up losing money on the product cost to fill the first box if the discount is really aggressive. It can work, but just be careful when doing this.

We ran a very aggressive offer in BusterBox in the past where the customer just paid £5 for the first box. We positioned it though that the first box was free, but the customer had to pay £5 shipping. This offer blew up, and we got thousands of new subscribers. We had to pay lots of attention to our numbers though through the lifetime of the offer to ensure it remained profitable (Which it did).

2. Free Gift

The free gift can work very well once it is actually a gift that your prospect is interested in. If it is some old stock down in your warehouse that you want to get rid of, performance will be terrible. That's why you need to offer something really, really cool which will grab attention and make people want to sign up for your subscription box on the spot.

A tip would be to try and source stuff that has a high perceived retail value but can be picked up for relatively cheap. Then lean on the value of the free gift in your marketing. This can make a big difference to the customer's perception and massively improve the conversion rate.

A great way to verify the demand for your free gift would be to head over to amazon and check how many reviews it has. If it looks like a popular product in your niche, you can tell it will probably work well as a gift with your box. An example of this would be when we were considering a GPS tracker for dogs as a free gift. We headed over to amazon and could see the brand we were going to use had thousands of reviews and looked extremely popular. We knew then it had the potential to work very well as a free gift. We were right. We launched the offer, and it sold out within a few days. Another way to verify demand would be to check Google keywords and see how many people are roughly searching for the product. If a lot of people are searching for it each month well, then it has a chance of working very well as a free gift.

The crazy thing is that not every item you think will be a hit works well. We have launched offers in the past that looked very promising even after lots of research, and they still flopped; when you get it right, though, the effect is pretty insane.

Here's an example:

We launched a free dog cooling mat for new subscribers right in the middle of summer. The sales completely blew up. The demand was crazy. We got the timing perfect, though, because it was right in the middle of a heatwave and everybody wanted to keep their dog cool. It also looked like a pretty fun product.

3. Double Your First Box For FREE

This offer can help to generate a lot of new subscribers once it is presented correctly. All you need to do is double the amount of stuff the customers get in the first box. This is very enticing for most consumers and also leaves a very good impression after the first delivery. Once you get this right, it can help a lot to improve your retention rate. The customers are so impressed with all the stuff they receive and the value you have provided they are not interested in cancelling. When we run this offer, the churn is always really low.

The only bad thing about this offer is it can cost a lot of money upfront to get all the stock in. So if you do decide to do it, make sure you keep on top of your cash flow, so you don't end up running into any issues. This offer can be a great way to clear excess stock, though. If you have stuff building up in your warehouse, run this offer to clear it all out and get a load of new customers in the process.

4. Theme Based Offers

If you do monthly themes for your box. Theme-based offers can work very well. You can reveal your theme ahead of time and base all your marketing material around that month's theme. You can also add one of the offers I mentioned above to improve your conversions even more.

So imagine you are sending out a safari box next month.

All your marketing material would be around this safari box, but then to make things even better, the first box has a deep discount, is double the amount of stuff, or has a really cool safari-based gift that fits the monthly theme

Example:

Imagine, during Christmas, you have a Christmas-based theme, with Christmas-based marketing, and on top of that, new customers can also double their first box as well. This is a very powerful offer that would sell very quickly.

Over time you will learn what your customers respond to by testing different offers and then tracking your metrics to make sure they are profitable. You will learn what works, and then you can make things a lot more interesting by adding different things and positioning them in different ways. If you can find a way to add digital products and other benefits that don't cost you a lot, this can also make a massive difference. This is because it raises the perceived value for the customer.

Offer Presentation.

It doesn't make a difference if you have the best offer in the world. If you don't know how to present it correctly, your sales will be slow. The biggest piece of advice I can give you is to hire a graphic designer to help you with this.

You are going to need professional stuff designed for your header, ads, and emails. Here are some tips to help you.

- **Header**

The offer should be displayed on the header of your website. It should be designed in a way that grabs attention but doesn't take away from your box. It needs to look extremely enticing. Professional pictures here are a must.

- **Emails**

Email marketing should be a big part of your marketing strategy. Your offer needs to be centre stage in all sales emails you send out. You should have many different versions of these emails so you can email your list regularly. Professional design work here makes a big difference.

- **Ads**

All ads that you send out should include the offer. The ads should be colourful. The subscription boxes should be packed with great products and the offer should be clear. Make the most of Facebook relaxing the 20% text rule and put your offer in bold text in each image. This will make a big difference for the placements where the caption isn't so easy to read. E.g., Instagram.

For unboxing video ads, the offer needs to be discussed by whoever is opening the box on camera. I can't stress this enough presentation is critical, so make sure you have the design skills to get it right, and if not, hire a freelancer or full-time graphic designer to help.

We place an enormous amount of time and resources into coming up with new offers in BusterBox. Usually, when we get stuck in the mud and sales aren't going well, the thing that gets us back on track is a fresh offer. One of the most frustrating things is when you think you are about to launch a hit offer, you do all the work, and it flops. We can pretty much tell when an offer is a flop after a few hours. If we send a sales email to our list and it doesn't perform, it usually means the offer isn't going to work. This isn't good when you have done all the work and ordered all the stock ahead of time. We have come up with a process to stop this from happening to us. I will share it with you below because it will save you a lot of time and hassle.

Rapid Subscription Box Offer Testing

You will do your offer research as normal and search for appealing products that you can pair with your first box to make it a no-brainer purchase for your customers. Once you have identified a product that you think may work, you then start the testing process.

- The first thing you do is head over to Amazon, and check to see if this product can be delivered through prime. You also need to ensure they have plenty of stock.
- You would duplicate your website onto a different URL and change the header to promote this offer.

- You would then send out an email to your list or a segment of your list, depending on how big it is promoting the offer.
- You would then check the response from that email. If it performed well and you got some sales, that is probably a winning offer.
- You would then send out your boxes and order the free gifts through amazon prime directly to your customer's houses.
- You would then shut down the offer straight away.
- You would then source the stock from a supplier and plan to launch that winning offer properly at a future date.

Now you might think I am completely crazy suggesting this, as it is going to be expensive to order free gifts through amazon prime. In our case, paying extra for this is completely worth it because we are buying speed. We can test offers quickly and verify demand without committing to a massive amount of work. If you are not comfortable doing this through amazon prime, you could always order a small amount of stock and test that way, but it does take longer when you do this.

Ideally, you want to find at least twelve high-converting offers for your Subscription Box and you want to plan them all out twelve months in advance. This will give you a massive advantage because you can order stock and plan out your marketing materials well in advance. Before we did this in BusterBox, we found there was a lot of start-stop involved with the growth of our company. We may be doing unbelievably well in one month. Then the offer would burn out, and we would be scrambling around looking for another winning offer, wasting time. This is not a good approach. You should have everything planned out twelve months in advance, and that way, you know once you have twelve converting offers, you are going to have a great year of growth in your business.

CHAPTER 10
Generating Traffic

You can have the most fantastic subscription box in the world with the most irresistible offer plastered all over your website, but if that site is a ghost town and nobody knows about it. You won't get any subscribers signed up or generate any revenue. If you want to grow a successful business, you need to be able to repeatedly drive a substantial amount of traffic to your website. A lack of repeatable and profitable traffic is one of the biggest obstacles which stops new subscription box owners in their tracks and kills their dreams.

Suppose your entire marketing plan revolves around posting organic content to your social media pages. In that case, I am afraid you must re-evaluate your strategy because you are heading for disappointment. I am afraid it is not 2012 anymore and organic reach is pretty much dead. For the majority of platforms, it's now pay-to-play, and if you are not willing to adapt to this, you are unlikely to get anywhere.

In this chapter, I will explain all the different ways of generating traffic and give you some advice so that when you launch your subscription box, you will have a game plan to make it a massive success.

Now the first thing to bear in mind is that Google ads can work unbelievably well for many different businesses (I know because I have used them successfully in the past for many projects). When it comes to using them to generate sales for a Subscription Box, they usually aren't the best option for many niches. This is because the Subscription Box model is still a relatively new concept, and there typically aren't many people Googling for your box because they don't even know what you do exists.

My business is in the dog niche, which is a big market. But the number of people searching for a dog subscription box each month on Google is small. It is growing all the time but is still very small. This doesn't mean that these people aren't potential customers. It just means they aren't aware they can sign up for a monthly box of toys and treats for their dog, so they aren't actively searching for us.

Now, you should still definitely test Google ads because there is a possibility they will work for you, and when they do work, they generate intent-based traffic, which is usually excellent quality. If your search volume is low, you can also try bidding on other keywords that potential customers may be searching for that fits your niche but isn't a direct search for your box and then trying to convert them to subscribers.

Now for the majority of Subscription Boxes, we are in the demand generation business. So we have to create our own demand and then use that demand to get subscribers signed up. That is another reason why direct response works so well for this business model. We can create irresistible offers and target ideal customers on platforms like Facebook and TIKTOK and get people to sign up, even though they had never heard of the concept before seeing the ad.

The example I would give to you would be a Basketball Subscription Box company.

There are probably very few searches each month for a Basketball Box. But suppose the owner of this imaginary Business started running Facebook ads and targeted people interested in Basketball with an Irresistible offer. In that case, there is a good chance they would generate demand and get many people signed up for the box.

Obviously, there are exceptions to this, and there are certainly opportunities to incorporate Google ads into your overall strategy, but for most boxes, what I just wrote is reality.

Now that I have made that clear, let's break down the three different kinds of traffic.

1. Traffic You Own

This is the best kind of traffic because it's the most profitable by far and the only traffic you have full control over. This kind of traffic is made up of different assets you collect in your business, with the most obvious being your email list. Email accounts for a gigantic amount of our sales in BusterBox. It's incredibly profitable because once we collect the customer's email address, we don't need to pay to reach them again. They may sign up for a subscription and then purchase additional gifts for their friend's dogs or their dog from our email marketing at Christmas. They may also cancel at some point but then reactivate their subscription in the future after seeing one of our sales emails.

We have full control over this traffic. When we send an email blast, we get a lot of traffic over to our site immediately for free and start making sales. You don't get this from any other kind of traffic. It is also an insurance policy, as there are so many horror stories of social media accounts getting shut down, SEO getting wiped out, or Facebook groups getting closed. I hope that never happens to you, but if it does, they can't take your email list away from you, and you are in a solid position to build everything back up quickly.

Another example of traffic you own would be a list of phone numbers. Sending an SMS blast is a very effective way of reaching leads and driving sales. It is similar to email, but the open rate is usually a lot higher the downside is you have to pay to do this compared to email, which is free.

2. Traffic You Control

You don't own this traffic but can control it and tell it where to go. This is any traffic that is generated by using paid ads. I am talking about paying to drive traffic from platforms such as Facebook, Google, YouTube, TikTok, Snap, Pinterest, etc. When you run traffic from any of these platforms, you don't own the traffic. The platform does, but you control it by running ads and sending visitors who click your ads where you want.

The only downside to this is that you obviously have to pay to run ads on these platforms and are only a guest. You have no control over rules or ad prices and can have your ad account shut down for basically nothing. (Trust me, it happens more than you think and there are so many horror stories of people losing their entire business when it does)

The benefit of this kind of traffic is it is rapid. You can start advertising your box, putting your offer in front of the right people, and generating sales within a few hours if you know what you're doing. This makes it very attractive, and for the majority of businesses, if you want to get anywhere, you need to accept the fact that you will have to run paid traffic

3. Traffic You Earn / Traffic You Don't Control

This is the kind of traffic that you don't control. It usually comes via organic means. This could be from search engines, a blog post, or word of mouth. Again, it is hard to control this traffic. It just appears on your website, and it isn't easy to verify where it came from or where it ends up going. Don't get me wrong, it is fantastic when it happens and starts generating sales, but it's tough to predict when it will occur, so it normally isn't something you can depend on each day to drive new subscribers.

Example: One of your customers mentions your website on their Instagram page. Then one of their followers sees the post and heads to your website. You have no control over that sequence of events. Hence, it can be called "Traffic you don't control."

In some instances, this can be classified as "Earned traffic" because you have to work to get this traffic. – Writing a blog post, posting regularly on social media, or getting ranked for certain search terms on Google all require work.

Russell Brunson initially broke down the different kinds of traffic in this manner. I thought it was a very clever way of doing it, making it extremely easy to understand. I recommend checking out his book Traffic Secrets, which is excellent for anybody looking to grow an online business.

Now the aim of the game is to convert as much traffic as possible into traffic you own. The best way to achieve this is to have some way of capturing a visitor's email address on your website; when you have an email list that is always growing with fresh leads, it naturally brings down your customer acquisition cost and enables you to generate a lot of traffic and sales pretty much at will.

Now let's break down all the different ways of generating traffic and sales.

1. Influencers

Influencer marketing can be a cheap way to generate traffic and sales when you first set up your business. These influencers can be spread across platforms such as YouTube, Instagram, Snapchat, TikTok, and others. It doesn't matter what platform it is. All of them have the potential to work once the influencer you have picked out has a following which matches your target demographic.

I like going the YouTube route with influencers, and I will explain why. The videos on YouTube last forever, and they have the potential to keep working and making sales for your business long into the future. At the same time, the other platforms usually offer more of a quick boost of sales. Take Instagram, for example. Once the Instagram story has disappeared, and the influencer has made a few more posts to their profile, the post promoting your box loses a lot of its selling power as nobody new is looking at it.

Anyway, the platform doesn't matter. Any of these platforms will work once you find the right influencer. I would recommend researching your niche deeply and then creating a list of the best influencers. You can use a tool such as Social Blade to verify these are legitimate influencers and that they aren't buying fake followers. You should also look at the engagement they get on each post. If they have a massive following but only get a few likes on a post-it isn't a good idea to work with them.

When you are only starting, it is usually better to focus on micro-influencers. These people don't have massive followings (Usually a few thousand) but have a significant influence over their followers and great engagement. It is usually much cheaper to work with these people, or they will be happy to post for you in exchange for a free box, and that is it. Then, when you get bigger and have the cash flow, you can consider working with some of the bigger influencers. Just always be wary of the cost involved when you do this. Some of them charge a small fortune to promote your box.

We were quoted £20,000 for a YouTube video from somebody with a couple hundred thousand subscribers. So when we worked out how many new customers we would have had to get from that video to make it worthwhile, we could easily see that it would never have been viable.

When you reach out to influencers, the best approach is from a direct response perspective. That means you should always let them promote whatever offer you are running on your website, and you should also make it time sensitive with a deadline.

Here's an example

Imagine you own a Cat Subscription Box and are running an offer where new subscribers will receive a free Cat bed. You would send this entire package to the chosen influencers and ask them to mention to their followers that if they sign up before a specific date, they will receive a free cat bed with their first box.

When you do something like this, it is important to track where the sales are coming from, so you can see which influencers are the most effective and driving the most sign-ups. The easiest way to track this is to give each influencer their unique coupon code or you can consider using a piece of software such as Rewardful.

In my experience, you normally only get three effective posts from each influencer before the number of sales they bring in decreases significantly. This is because their entire following is familiar with your box by the time they get to the 4th box you send them to promote. This means you must consistently be on the lookout for new influencers to promote your box so you can continue using this channel for maximum sales. However, it is a good way of getting sales through, and it is also a relatively low-risk way of promoting your box as a lot of the time, it will only cost you a free box, and that's it.

2. Organic Social Media

I think the days of driving a massive amount of sales via organic social media are pretty much dead on the majority of platforms. At the time of writing this, TikTok still has an enormous organic reach, but eventually, that will die out as more users and content gets pushed to the platform. When a new social media platform comes out, there is always a small window of opportunity where you can get a lot of organic reach. It happened with Facebook, Instagram, and now TikTok. Eventually, though, so many users are putting out content that the reach gets decreased, and it turns into Pay to Play if you want to get any traction.

Now that doesn't mean you shouldn't be active across social media. On the contrary, it is essential to have your business present on all the big platforms. There are a few different reasons why you need to do this.

- **It Gives Your Brand Credibility**

A lot of the time, before somebody signs up to your box, they will want to check out your Instagram page, your TikTok account, or your Facebook business page. If they see you regularly posting content and interacting with your followers, it gives your brand credibility as a legitimate company, improving social proof.

- **It Can Lead To Sales**

Even though the organic reach is dead on many of these platforms, you can still pick up some sales from posting organically. We have found it in BusterBox. People love to engage with our content even if they are not ready to buy from us. Dog lovers will hang out on our page and enjoy the stuff we are posting, and then when it comes to the point where they need to make a purchase for their dog, we are top of mind, and they sign up.

- **It Can Help With Paid Ads**

At the time of writing this, there is a theory that posting regularly to your Facebook business page and getting good engagement can actually lower the price of your paid advertising with them. This is because they see you are a real business that is putting out quality content that people engage with and then give you a slightly lower CPM price to reward you.

I have heard this multiple times, and I tend to believe it because what I have noticed is when a new business starts advertising on Facebook with a new business page and little content and engagement, the CPM price is generally through the roof.

It would be best if you were consistent when posting on these platforms, and the best way to do this is by planning your content ahead of time. For example, in BusterBox, we produce helpful dog tips, borrow memes and put up pictures of dogs enjoying our boxes. We use a program called Later to schedule all of our content a couple of weeks in advance. I recommend you do the exact same, as it will save you a lot of time and hassle in the long run.

3. Email Swaps

This is a highly underrated way of generating traffic and sales for your Subscription Box. It became apparent to us that this channel could be effective when we had several subscription boxes getting in touch with us enquiring about doing this. These were some of the biggest subscription boxes in the UK, which weren't competitors, but they were targeting similar demographics as ourselves.

The way it works is the following. We send out a few emails to our email list promoting their Subscription Box in exchange for them doing the exact same thing for us. If you have a strong offer, this can work exceptionally well, and you can get a lot of sales via this channel.

4. Insert Swaps

This is very similar to email swaps, but you are swapping inserts with other companies instead of emails. It can work exceptionally well because, with this kind of marketing, you are getting close to a 100% open rate. E.g., everybody will open their box, and the vast majority will read all materials in the box. If you partner with a subscription box or a straight e-commerce company that isn't a competitor but targets the same demographic as you, this can get a lot of sales and be a win-win for both companies.

5. SEO

We have managed to rank very well with SEO, mainly due to one key factor. We have a lot of high-quality backlinks from sites with a lot of authority. This is because we have been featured in many news articles, review sites, and high-quality blogs. I recommend you do similar in your business. It takes time to build up these backlinks, but it is worth it long term.

6. Facebook Groups

Facebook groups can be a compelling and cheap way to grow your Subscription Box Business. I highly recommend creating one for your brand and putting effort into developing it. It can take a bit of time at the start to get the ball rolling, but once you get to five-hundred members or so and you have good engagement, then Facebook will start automatically pushing new members into your group. This can eventually result in your group growing on auto-pilot, giving you a lot of free leads that you can then turn into subscribers.

When you create your group at the start, you should invite any of your friends whom you think would be a good fit for it. Then you should join similar groups in your niche and provide as much value as possible. People will naturally gravitate towards you and visit your profile or add you as a friend. You can then invite those people into your group. It can take a bit of time, but if you keep doing this, eventually, you will grow your group to the level where Facebook will take over and start sending new members automatically.

You shouldn't try to sell your box all the time in your group, though. Instead, you should keep providing value and helping people and occasionally come up with an offer for your box. If you do this correctly, this can become a very cheap way of getting new subscribers.

7. Paid Traffic

This is my favourite way to advertise and get new subscribers signed up. This is because you can generate a lot of traffic and get a lot of sales quickly with paid traffic. When you get good at this, you have a lot of control over how quickly your company grows. Truthfully, I don't believe you have much of a business unless you have a repeatable, profitable, and scalable way of getting customers. For a lot of Subscription Boxes, paid traffic does this.

Unfortunately, it is impossible for me to explain how to run ads on every platform in this book. This is because the tactics are changing and evolving all the time. (If you want paid traffic training, head over to my Subscription Box Experts Program at

www.SubscriptionBoxExperts.com, and I have you covered) What I can do, though, is break down the core strategy, which never changes, which you can then apply and see massive results when running your ads.

My favourite platform to run paid ads on is Facebook. Facebook gets a lot of hate, but it is still the biggest social media platform by far and is normally the most effective advertising channel for most Subscription Boxes. This is because it has the most reach and advanced targeting options, which is normally the most cost-effective way of reaching your target customers. When setting up your ads through the Meta Business manager, you also get access to Instagram as a placement. This is also another highly effective platform for running Subscription Box Ads.

Another platform that is growing rapidly and we have had consider-able success is TikTok. They have put a lot of resources into developing their ad platform, and I have no doubt that it will be very close to matching Facebook in a few years. However, if you think TikTok is just a place for kids and teenagers to dance, I am afraid you are completely wrong. Older users are signing up for the app rapidly, and it is highly likely that your target customer is already using it or will be soon. So if you don't at least test running ads on it, you are leaving a lot of money on the table.

Now the first thing you want to do with any of these platforms is set up accurate tracking. It doesn't matter which one you are advertising on. A specific way of doing this for most of them will involve installing a pixel. A pixel is a piece of code you install on your website that tracks all user behaviour. This allows you to set up ads targeting specific events such as conversions, track performance, and make special audiences, such as custom audiences for retargeting or lookalike audiences for reaching new customers.

Let me explain if you don't know what a lookalike audience is. This is an audience that contains a group of people with similar characteristics to a list of people you have uploaded to the advertising platform.

Example:

You have a list of a thousand people who previously signed up for your subscription box. You export all of their email addresses and then upload them to Facebook to create a new custom audience. You then turn that custom audience into a lookalike audience. Facebook then uses that data to create a brand new audience of people with similar characteristics.

This is extremely powerful, and these audiences usually work extremely well for driving sales.

You can also make lookalike audiences of leads you collected, people who watched your videos, engaged with your ads, or visited your website. All of these audiences usually work pretty well as well.

Since the IOS updates, most of these platforms are also recommending you install a conversion API, which helps with tracking further. (I would also recommend doing this and also installing anything else new which has been released after I publish this book) I will briefly explain if you don't know what the IOS updates are. Apple released a new update for the iPhone in 2021, which enables users to opt out of tracking. Obviously, this was a big blow for platforms such as Facebook as their business model depends massively on collecting user data so they can show ads to the right people.

When this update came out, it was a big blow to any business running ads online as it became more expensive to acquire customers and more difficult to track everything accurately. The good news is, even though these updates made things more challenging, consumers' buying habits did not change, and once you understand marketing, you can still have a lot of success with paid traffic.

When you start running paid traffic, you will want to test different audiences before you start ramping up your budget. To do this, you should create some avatars of who your ideal customer is likely to be. First, you need to know their likely age range, gender, and then a few different things they are likely to be interested in. Then you simply test a few of these audiences and find the ones which convert the best.

Once you have a few audiences picked out to test, you will want to create some ads. First, I will explain a basic format to follow when creating video ads on Facebook, which usually works well.

Facebook loves videos. The algorithm goes crazy for a good video, and it is one of the easiest ways to lower the CPA. Don't worry though, you don't need to spend thousands on creating professional videos. Instead, we found the best videos that convert are the simple ones you can record on your phone, which are about thirty to forty seconds long.

So here's the magic format.

1. The customer receives the box and states what it is.
2. The customer opens the box and is ecstatic and slowly starts going through the products.

3. The customer says what the offer is. They take out the free gift and show it to the camera if it is a gift.
4. The customer says what good value the box is and states they are delighted they signed up (make sure it is one of the best boxes you have ever sent out and the products are all very high quality and the boxes look full).

That is honestly it. I know every niche is different, but I have seen this type of approach work time and time again with boxes. It really doesn't have to be complicated. This type of video can be recorded on most phones. No expensive cameras are required. To be honest with you, a phone is probably better anyway as it comes across as more authentic.

Who will do this for me?

We have thousands of people signed up, so we get videos from customers we use for this. Some of you will only be starting, so here are some solutions:

1. Get a box and go down to your friend's house. Ask them nicely to do the video for you and print out a script telling them exactly what to say.
2. Contact influencers on Instagram and tell them you will give them a free box if they shoot a video for you in the format described (micro-influencers are your best shot with this).
3. Run a competition for your subscribers and give away some free boxes for prizes. Tell everybody to enter the competition. They just need to send in their best box opening videos, and you will pick some winners.

Congratulations, You now have a selection of high-converting videos you can use for years in your marketing campaigns. All these videos can be tested to find the top converters (Who knows, maybe all of them will convert, and you can run them all at the same time, spread across cold and warm traffic, and clean up).

The exact same process can be applied to TikTok if you are running ads there. The only difference is the type of videos that convert on TikTok are very different from Facebook. TikTok's slogan is don't make ads, make TikToks. This is very true. You should study the platform to understand how it works and what kind of content is getting the most engagement.

Obviously, there are a million ways you can structure your videos and every niche can be a bit different. What I have explained above is a basic formula you can use, which is easy to make and can produce great results.

Images

Images are going to be another important part of the equation. I see so many ads from Subscription Boxes showing on my Facebook newsfeed, and the boxes look filled with a bunch of junk the owners got from a discount store. It's either that or the images are poor quality and dark, and it's hard to see what is in the box.

Here are some tips.

1. Get some professional pictures of your box. If you don't have the skill to do this, just hire somebody. If you don't want to hire somebody, purchase a light box from Amazon, which will help your box look a lot better in photos.

2. Make sure the box looks full and it is a colourful setting, so it grabs attention on the newsfeed. (Take a look at any of the ads for any of the big subscription boxes to get inspiration)
3. Never do any ads with a closed box (This is a sure-fire way to send your ad costs through the roof)
4. Take advantage of the new rule on Facebook, where you can now add more than 20% of text to your images. You should have whatever offer you are running as big and bold text on the images. This is because it won't be easy to see the ad copy on some of the placements, so this can be a great way of grabbing attention and giving your ad some context.

Writing ads that convert.

There are many different things to learn when it comes to writing compelling copy, but it simply would not be possible for me to teach them all to you in this book. So instead, I can teach you a straightforward formula that can be used to write high-converting Subscription Box Ads.

You should break down the copy when creating your ads into the following sections.

- **Pattern Interrupt:** (Make a statement to grab the prospect's attention. BOOM! Calling All Cat Lovers! Attention Gym Lover, etc.)
- **Offer:** Hit them with your unbelievable offer (You can now get 50% off your first box etc.)
- **Tell Them What You Do:** (MagicCrate is a monthly delivery of crazy and unique magic tricks that will blow your friends and family away)

- **Social Proof** (Over 5,000 people can't be wrong)

This is an effortless way to structure your ads. It can get a lot more complicated, but if you are only learning how to advertise I would advise following the above layout. A lot of work goes into copywriting, and it isn't something you can learn overnight. I find for cold traffic, a shorter copy straight to the point works better. For retargeting, long form copy can work very well as you fight each customer's objection.

Headlines:

Just keep it simple. Come up with five different headlines, test each, and see which one converts the best. We have found that your ads typically convert way better if you put your offer in the headline

1. Double Your First Box For FREE.
2. Get a $60 gift with sign up
3. Get two boxes for $20
4. Join today and get an extra month FREE
5. Get your first box FREE (just pay p&p)

Call to action.

All we use are one of the following call to actions. Sign up or learn more. That is literally it.

This is a simple crash course on how to lay your ads out. This is usually a big problem for many people when they start, and they tend to get overwhelmed. My advice is to keep it as simple as possible and logically work through each step of the process, and eventually, you will find ads that convert. An important thing to remember is you need to do a lot of testing. You simply won't find working ads overnight. So you need to have patience and test everything.

This is very true when you are only getting started. However, as time progresses and you get better at creating offers and ads, it becomes much easier to launch new ads that convert pretty quickly as you eventually learn exactly what your potential customers want.

When you are running ads on TikTok, the amount of copy that is required is a lot less. You only get a tiny section; this usually is where we list our offer, and that is it. TikTok is different because all the selling is done through a video.

A big tip is that before you start running paid traffic, you should study other companies' ads in your niche. You can use something called the Facebook ad library to do this. You simply type in the name of any company you want, and you will be able to see all of their active ads running on Facebook and Instagram. In addition, you can see exactly when a company started running any particular ad. If the ad has been running for a considerable amount of time well, then that ad is highly likely to be profitable. This will give you a perfect idea of the ads converting in your niche. This should hopefully give you some inspiration, cut down your learning, and help you get a profitable campaign up and running ASAP.

CHAPTER 11
Follow Up Marketing

There is a lot of money and new subscribers in the follow-up. If you're in charge of a company that is afraid to follow up effectively, you are putting your business at a massive disadvantage. Not everybody will be ready to purchase from you immediately when they come across your ads, and it is your job as a subscription box owner to follow up with those prospects and overcome any objection which is stopping them from becoming a subscriber.

I will give you an example.

A potential customer is on the bus on the way to work. They are browsing the internet, and they come across one of your ads. This prospect is very excited at the thought of signing up for your box, but it is not convenient for them to pull out their credit card on the bus and sign up then and there. They say to themselves, when they finish work and get home, the first thing they are going to do is sign up. The problem is humans have a million different things going on at any one time, and signing up for your subscription is probably at the bottom of the pile. In an ideal world, this person will sign up for this box when they get home, but unfortunately, it isn't an ideal world, and they will probably forget your company exists.

If you have no way to follow up with this person, congratulations, you just wasted money on the original ad, and you also lost out on a new subscriber. You need a strong follow-up process in place to stop things like this from happening, and thankfully because of the times we are living in, technology allows us to do this relatively easily.

Let's go through some examples.

1. Email

The most obvious and easiest way to follow up is by email and It doesn't cost you anything, so it makes a lot of sense. There are a few different ways you can collect a visitor's email address.

Email collection examples

- A pop-up on your website where you exchange something for the email (discount code, lead magnet)
- The email collection point could be built into your signup flow
- You could gamify it by using something called Wheelio (The customer can enter their email to spin a wheel for the chance to win a prize)

Once we have collected a visitor's email address, we have a 5-day sequence set up to fire if the customer hasn't already purchased. The emails range from showing different offers, giving specific discounts, and sending personal letters from the owner's dog asking why they haven't signed up yet. This mixture of emails works very well and we get a lot of people signed up from this sequence. I would recommend implementing something similar into your business.

A great piece of advice I can give you is to create a burner email and then sign up for the mailing list of all the big boxes and leading e-commerce companies in your space. You will then see first-hand what these companies are doing via email, and it should give you a lot of ideas that you can implement in your business. You will be able to learn what kind of creatives are converting and what kind of frequency the emails are getting sent. That is what we did in Buster Box. We literally signed up to twenty different companies lists which we knew were doing well, and then built our entire email strategy from what we learned.

2. SMS

SMS marketing is another great way to follow up. This is because the open rates with SMS are extremely high compared to email. The only downside is that SMS isn't free and you actually need to pay to send text messages. That's why it is very important that you monitor this channel closely to make sure what you are doing is profitable.

We use SMS to follow up with cancelled customers when we launch a new offer because it normally wins some of them back. We only do this kind of SMS blast once a month at most, though. Otherwise, you can end up really annoying people if you are texting them too frequently. We also use SMS marketing for flash sales in our store. We have found this works great, and when we do this, we include current customers as well. A good example of this is when we run a sale on dog beds. This always performs well for us and generates a lot of additional revenue.

3. Direct Mail

Direct mail can be extremely effective for following up with cancelled subscribers and trying to win them back. You already have their address details, and this is a great channel to grab their attention that not many other companies will be using. It is not expensive to put together a campaign like this. If you have an offer which you think has the potential to win a good percentage of them back, you should do it. One of the most effective ways of doing this is by putting a QR code on the postcard. Then when they scan this, it will direct them to a page where they can sign back up and unlock the offer you are advertising.

I would highly recommend testing this if you have been running a while and you have a lot of old customer data sitting there being unused. This has the potential to turn into a gold mine for your business.

4. Phone Follow Up

Picking up the phone and calling your cancelled subscribers can be a great way of winning them back. A lot of the time when I suggest this, nobody is keen to do it. I understand this completely. It is time-consuming, and if you end up speaking to somebody who doesn't have something nice to say about your business, it can hurt. I still recommend you do it because those conversations can not only help win people back but will also be filled with a lot of valuable information which you can use to improve your business.

Back in the very early days of BusterBox, we used to spend a lot of time on the phone speaking to cancelled customers. We would find out why they cancelled, and then we would fix their issue and try and win them back.

Example:

We discovered a proportion of people were cancelling because they had a lot of dog toys and dog treats building up, or they simply couldn't afford the subscription anymore. We decided to launch BusterBox lite pretty much immediately, which was a cheaper and smaller version of our box with fewer products. We then started calling all of these people who cancelled because of the reasons mentioned above and told them we had a solution and asked if they would be interested in trying it. We ended up getting 80% of them signed back up to the service on a cheaper subscription. We then incorporated BusterBox lite into our cancellation process to help reduce the churn for any future customers that cancelled.

You should do the exact same in your business. Especially if you are only getting started and don't have many customers, put aside some time every week to call your customers and ex-customers and find out how you can improve your business and how you can win some of them back by solving their issues.

5. Retargeting Ads

I am going to share a retargeting strategy that can be used to seriously boost your ROI when advertising via Facebook or some other paid channels. We have used this exact strategy to sign up thousands of new subscribers in BusterBox and keep the CPA down as well. This works really well in a Subscription Box, but it will also work with pretty much any business. I think it would be especially effective if you were selling high-ticket courses and would help to get a lot of customers through your door.

A key element of any successful Facebook marketing campaign will heavily involve setting up your retargeting correctly. If you don't know what that means, let me explain.

A retargeting campaign is what happens after somebody visits your website and doesn't buy straight away. They should then see some follow-up ads which will push them to sign up for your box. When somebody sees your ad and comes over to your website, it's clear they have some level of interest in what you are doing and could potentially end up signing up.

What stops them is usually down to a few different factors.

1. It isn't convenient to buy

The example I used at the start of the chapter about the person on the bus who saw your ad explains this perfectly. Even though they saw your ad and headed over to your website with a level of interest, it isn't convenient for them to sign up then and there. This person could be an ideal customer, but their current situation is stopping them from buying.

2. They aren't ready to buy

A potential customer may have seen your ad and is really impressed with what you do and has a genuine interest in becoming a customer at some point, but they just aren't ready right now. This is perfectly normal and is actually pretty common as well. When circumstances change, though, there is a high possibility this person will eventually sign up.

3. There is something stopping them

This is usually the most common reason why somebody does not sign up for your box. They saw your ad, and they headed over to your website with some level of interest in signing up. Then once they landed on your website, something happened that presented them with an objection which stopped them from making the purchase.

This could be down to price, lack of trust, lack of understanding, or doubts about the quality of your box or service.

When any of these things happen, it is your job as a subscription box owner/marketer to follow up with the customer and fight their objections and get them to pull out their credit card and sign up for your box.

Here's how the typical retargeting campaign looks

1. Somebody visits your website
2. They don't convert
3. You start retargeting them, and they see your ads everywhere they go all over the internet
4. The ad is static, and nine times out of ten, it is a rehash of the cold traffic ad you used to originally target them
5. You don't put much thought into this part of your advertising, but you see some cheap sales, so you are happy (Most of the time at low volume)

I am afraid this is a very poor way to set up your retargeting campaigns, and if you are doing it, then you are probably leaving thousands of dollars on the table. What you need to understand is people are different, and each person will have their own reasons as to why they didn't initially sign up. If you don't find a way of fighting all of the main objections, then a large percentage of those people who see your retargeting ads will never end up signing up for your box.

This is what I recommend doing instead.

The first thing you need to do is figure out what the main objections are which are stopping people from signing up. A good place to start is to look at your cancellation reasons. Usually, the same reasons why people are cancelling are the same objections which are stopping them from signing up in the first place.

In BusterBox, here are some of the main reasons preventing people from joining.

- They are afraid the toys are poor quality and the dog won't like them
- They are unsure about the quality of the treats
- They think the dog may not like the items in the box
- They don't trust our company yet to commit to a subscription

Once these reasons became clear to us, I then went ahead and created a retargeting campaign which addressed all of these objections in each ad.

Here's an example of the copy in one of the ads, which is

targeted to people who are afraid to sign up in case the toys are of poor quality.

One of the main questions we get is what kind of toys do you use, and are they suitable for your dog?
Well, the answer is we have a massive selection of cool and unique toys to satisfy every kind of dog breed.
We pack our boxes with funky plush toys, fun rubber toys, and engaging puzzle toys each month.
Sign up now and bring happiness to your dog every single month.

The creative was a slide show which went through a selection of all of our best toys so potential customers could see for themselves how good they are. This ad converted like crazy because we addressed one of the biggest objections head-on and showed customers that their dogs would love our toys.

Another example would be the following.

This ad is targeted at people who won't join up because they think the treats aren't good enough quality for their dog.

You're probably wondering what kind of treats come in a BusterBox.
Each box comes with high-quality, all-natural treats suitable for your dog, from handy, tasty snacks to meaty chews that dogs love to munch.
Each treat is sourced from reputable suppliers in the UK, Ireland, and the E.U Made with the finest ingredients and processes. 100% natural and healthy, Grain FREE and hypoallergenic options are available.
Sign up now and bring happiness to your dog every single month.

The ad creative was a picture of five happy dogs enjoying their BusterBoxes and the healthy treats which came in them.

This was another ad which converted really well because we addressed this objection head-on again. Potential customers love their dogs, and they want to ensure they are getting the best quality treats. Once we assured them this would be the case with BusterBox, anybody who was on the fence ended up signing up.

I urge you to take inspiration from this and do the exact same thing when setting up your retargeting campaigns in your own Subscription Box Business. Remember, the messaging your cold traffic and warm traffic get should be completely different.

- Your cold traffic ads are designed to grab attention with your irresistible offer and get as many people signed up as possible.
- Your retargeting/warm traffic ads should be designed to follow up with people who are already aware of your business but have an objection. It is your job to fight these objections and get them signed up.

If you follow this advice, it will improve the performance of your marketing campaigns massively and will help you get a lot more people signed up for your subscription box.

CHAPTER 12
Subscription Box Churn

When you first launch your Subscription Box business, the main thing you will be focused on will be acquiring new customers. This is perfectly normal, and we were the exact same in BusterBox. We were under the impression at the very start that if we just figured out how to repeatedly get customers, we would have a very successful business. Unfortunately, this isn't the case at all. The most important metric in any subscription business is churn. It does not matter what kind of subscription business you have either. Your churn rate will play a massive factor in how successful and profitable your business turns out.

There are so many different strategies and tactics you can use to get customers signed up, but if you haven't figured out how to keep them, you are fighting a losing battle. After running your business for a short period of time, you will realise how true this is. There is nothing more frustrating than investing a lot of time and money into a big marketing push and then realising after a couple of months that a large percentage of those customers have cancelled.

In case you don't know what churn is, let me explain it in the most simple terms.

Subscription churn is the number of Subscribers that stop paying for your Subscription Box in a given period of time. E.g. They cancel their subscription or their card fails and can't be charged.

When it comes to Subscription Boxes, the most common period to measure it would be on a monthly basis with the following formula.

You would simply divide the number of people who cancelled during a 30-day time period by the number of active users you started with for that time period.

The percentage that comes from that calculation would then be your monthly churn rate.

Customer churn rate formula

(Cancelled Customers in the last 30 days / Active Customer 30 days ago) x 100

Example. A 10% churn rate means that 10% of the total subscribers you had 30 days ago have cancelled within the last 30 days)

Now I personally do not recommend tracking your churn manually, as mistakes can happen. Plus, you have no reason to do this when there is software that will do it for you. The Subscription Box platform you choose may do it, or you can sign up for a piece of software such as ChartMogul, Baremetrics, or Profitwell. Any of these will give you a full breakdown of your churn rate plus all the other Subscription metrics you need to be tracking (More on that in a later chapter).

What is a good churn rate?

Now, this is a question that comes up time and time again when I am speaking to Subscription Box owners. They want to know if they have a good churn rate or do they need to be worried about the direction their company is heading. The truth is, you should be working to reduce your churn rate consistently, as it isn't something which will ever go away. You will always have a percentage of customers who will cancel, and you will be working to reduce that percentage throughout the entire lifetime of your business.

As a general rule of thumb, you should be aiming to have a monthly churn rate of 10% or under in your Subscription Box. I haven't just pulled this figure out of thin air. There is a reason behind this. If you were running a SaaS company (software as a service), a monthly churn rate of 10% would be considered terrible for a lot of products. With a direct-to-consumer subscription, it is a bit different, and the churn will always be higher. This is because people will eventually reach a point where they want to cancel the subscription.

This could be down to a number of reasons; I will give you one in BusterBox, which can never be solved. If somebody's dog eventually passes away, the owner will cancel the subscription. This is a terrible time in any pet owner's life, and it is completely understandable why they need to cancel. There is nothing we can do as a company in this instance to save the customer, and we would never try to. We just show compassion for their loss and wish them well.

For the majority of SaaS companies, it will be lower because you are selling your subscription to a business, and they actually need to keep paying so they can access the software and continue to function. E.g. your email platform. You aren't ever going to cancel that once they provide good service as you need to use it every day. When you are selling your Subscription Box directly to a person, it is a bit different, and things do come up in people's lives which will force them to cancel, no matter how good your product or service is.

A 10% monthly churn rate or lower is very achievable, though, for a subscription box, if you have product market fit and people really see value in what you're doing. Obviously, it depends on your business, but if your churn rate is much higher, it can become difficult to keep growing or ensure your business is profitable.

I gave an example of this briefly back in Chapter 3 but let's touch on it again to remind you how important it is.

Imagine you had ten thousand active subscribers in your business.

Well, if this was the case and you had a 10% churn rate, well, then you would be losing a thousand subscribers a month.

So, just to stay where you are, you would need to sign up a thousand new customers a month.

This is doable but can be challenging if you have a very niche product with a small market.

Now imagine you had a churn rate of 20%. Well, in this case, you would need to get 2000 new subscribers signed up every single month just to stay where you are.

This is way more difficult to repeat over and over again, and eventually, you will find yourself under a lot of pressure.

It will also send your marketing bill through the roof and may mean your business will never be sustainable or profitable.

In an ideal scenario, you want to aim to get your monthly churn rate down to 5% - 8%, as this will make your entire business more profitable and easier to scale.

If your churn rate was 5% well, then at 10,000 active subscribers, you would only need to get 500 new subs a month to stay where you are.

This reduces your marketing cost significantly and means you will actually continue to grow at that level and not end up on a Subscription Treadmill.

Subscription Treadmill

Let me explain what a Subscription Treadmill is in case you don't know. This is when you reach a certain number of active subscribers and can't grow any higher because you can no longer outrun your churn rate.

E.g. You have two thousand active subscribers, and your monthly churn rate is 15%.

This means you need three hundred new subscribers every month just to stay where you are.

Now imagine the niche you are in is very small, and you don't have the marketing skill to get any more than three hundred subscribers per month, so you are now stuck on two thousand active subscribers.

You can still have a profitable business once the number of subscribers you get stuck on is past the breakeven point in your business. But I have witnessed some companies getting stuck on the treadmill while still burning money. This is a very scary place to be, and it usually means one thing when it happens. Your churn rate is way too high in your business for it ever to be sustainable and profitable.

Your churn rate is everything, and anybody who tries to tell you otherwise knows nothing about running a subscription business and is completely ignorant of basic maths. If you are trying to raise investment for your company and you speak to any private investor or VC, one of the first questions they will ask is what is your churn rate. If that number is too high, then they will walk away from any potential deal immediately because they know it will be nearly impossible to build value into the business if the churn rate is too high.

Anybody I know who has achieved amazing success in their subscription box business has a good churn rate. When you are getting started, it may be possible to outrun a bad churn rate for a period of time, but eventually, it will catch up with you, and you will hit that treadmill. When you do hit the treadmill, you need to ensure you are at a level where you are passed the breakeven point in your business and are actually producing profit; otherwise, you will go out of business fast.

Different Kinds Of Churn

There are two different kinds of churn that you will come across in any Subscription Business. Let me break them down.

1. Active Churn

This is also known as voluntary churn. This is the kind of churn you are probably most aware of. This takes place when the customer decides to cancel their subscription simply because they don't want your product anymore. This could be due to a number of reasons. But the main thing to remember is the customer went out of their way to cancel.

2. Passive Churn

This is also known as involuntary churn. This is when the customer does want to continue with their subscription but is unable to due to something stopping them. Both types of churn are equally important to attack as both will eat away at your profit margins, and you should have processes in place to fight each one.

Passive churn is easier to fight compared to active churn due to one important factor. Your customers actually want to continue with the subscription.

The majority of passive churn is caused by issues with the customers' payment method. The customer might lose their card, get a new card, change bank account, stop getting paid into a particular account etc. Any of these scenarios can result in the customer not being able to continue with their subscription unless you find a way to reach out and help them.

I came across a quote from Profit Well that states up to 40% of Subscription churn is down to passive churn.

I don't know what yours is in your business, but if it is anything close to that number, you have a big opportunity to reduce your overall churn and make your entire business more profitable. Remember what I said above? The customers actually want to continue with the subscription, so to reduce your churn, all you have to do is put processes in place to allow them to.

The first thing you need to do is make sure you have some sort of dunning email sequence set up where the customer can update their card details easily. Your email sequence should fire automatically when the customer's payment fails and should contain a link the customer can click to update their card in one click.

The ability for the customer to update their card in one click is really important.

If it's a case you have been sending emails advising the customer to log into their account and update their card there, you need to change that.

This is down to a couple of different factors.

1. The customer may not be able to navigate their account to update their card.
2. The customer may have forgotten their login details.

The whole point of this so to make the experience as simple as possible for the customer and remove any barrier which is preventing the customer from updating their card details.

Then more emails should be sent out automatically for the remainder of the failed attempts on the customers' cards. You should edit these emails and explain clearly to the customer if they need help updating their card, they can get in touch with you.

Our dunning sequence is set up over fifty days. This means if a customer's payment has failed, we will attempt to recover them for fifty days, and then if we can't do it, we will automatically cancel the subscription. The reason why we do this is that we have tested it, and we have found that if the customer does not come back in fifty days, it is highly unlikely they will ever make another payment again for that subscription.

You can also incorporate SMS into your dunning sequence and try and recover payments via text. The only thing I would say about that, though, is even though it can be effective due to the high open rate, it costs you money to send. So if you do add this option to your business, make sure you monitor the cost so you fully understand if it is worth it or not.

Dunning sequences are great, and they 100% make a big difference. But they aren't going to catch everybody. Sometimes the only way to stop a customer from churning out of your service is to pick up the phone and give them a call. Now I fully understand this is not viable for every business, but this is something you should seriously consider testing to see what kind of impact it makes. After all your renewals go through, you will be able to clearly see which customers failed due to card problems.

You can introduce yourself on the call and get some feedback about your service. Then tell them you would hate it if they missed the next box and ask whether they need assistance updating their card. This is a great way to kill two birds with one stone. You can get valuable feedback about your business and reduce your churn at the same time. Now obviously, this becomes more challenging as you scale up and you have more customers to call. You should still test it, though and see if it will be worth it for your business. If it turns out to make a big impact, then you can get your customer service team to take care of it each month.

Churn is the number one killer of so many subscription businesses, so you need to be smart and look at all the ways you can reduce it consistently.

Reducing Active Churn

One thing that I need to make clear is. It does not matter what processes you have in place to fight active churn. If you have a poor product that doesn't have product market fit, your business will always have a high churn rate. Once you find product market fit and people see the value in your box and get genuinely excited about receiving it, then it is not difficult to lower your churn.

Here are some tips which will help.

1. Solve the main drivers of churn and add solutions to your cancellation saver

The best way to reduce your churn rate is by looking at your data and identifying the biggest problems which are driving it up. Then you should come up with solutions to fix those problems. All the other stuff I mention later in the chapter will help, but if you don't fix the real problems, you are wasting your time. You can identify the biggest drivers of churn by sending a survey to everybody when they cancel and asking why are they leaving. Once you know what the biggest reasons are, then you need to come up with solutions and add them to your cancellation saver.

- **I will give you an example.**

One of the biggest reasons why people cancel BusterBox is because the dog is destroying the toys too quickly. This really annoys some people and makes them feel like they are not getting value for money. We came up with a simple solution to fix this. When somebody wants to cancel because of this, we will automatically upgrade them to receive stronger dog toys. This has made a massive dent in our overall churn because we have simply eliminated one of the biggest reasons why people cancel. You need to do the exact same in your business, and then when you're sure your solutions work, you should add them to an automatic cancellation saver to catch people when they try and cancel.

I would highly recommend spending some time signing up for some of the bigger subscription services and then trying to cancel, and you will get some very good ideas on how to structure your cancellation saver.

2. Get people to commit to a longer subscription

This is something which will have a massive impact immediately. I wouldn't recommend pushing people to sign up for your rolling one-month subscription. Obviously, it depends on your business, but for the vast majority, this will lead to a higher churn rate. I would advise incentivising people to commit to longer terms instead. You can do this by making your six and twelve month subscriptions cheaper and putting all your intro offers on them. That means if a customer signs up and tries to claim one of your offers, they can only get it if they commit for six or twelve months.

If you set your business up like this, after a while, you will be delighted to find out that the majority of customers are now committed for six or twelve months. This is exactly what we do in BusterBox, and 95% of our customers are committed to long-term plans. This normally means you will have way lower churn throughout your entire business.

3. Make your subscription essential

This will be very helpful for anybody that is in the early stage of setting up their business. If possible, make sure your product is needed in the customers' lives every day. In 2016, Dollar Shave Club was acquired by Unilever for 1 Billion Dollars. Do you know how they managed to get sold for such a large sum? A big part of the reason is their metrics actually make sense, AKA a low churn rate. They don't have a subscription where everybody leaves after a few months. Their Razors actually solve a problem as most men shave, and on top of that, their service is really good value and convenient. This is a winning formula, and my guess is they have a ridiculously low churn rate. I would imagine under 5%

So if you are starting out, you should consider doing something similar. If you focus on the replenishment model and nail that with a very strong brand and world-class service, you are sure to be onto a winning business.

If you are already up and running, why don't you look at launching another subscription that will run side by side with your main one? This is what we did a few years ago. We launched a complimentary subscription in the exact same niche. The only difference is this was an essential replenishment product. This worked out very well for us and helped to bring our churn down. All we did was simply contact all of our existing and previous customers and tell them about our new service. We got lots of people signed up this way and didn't have to pay any additional marketing costs. All that happened was we boosted our CLTV Considerably. (This won't always be possible for your niche, but it is worth looking into)

4. Create a community

A customer is going to hear from you twice a month. The first time is when their renewal goes through. The second time is when their box arrives. This is why you need to make your product more than just a box. If you make your customers feel like they are part of something, they are less likely to cancel.

Here are some ways you can do this.

- **Create a Facebook Group** – Make sure you are very active in the group. You should be promoting good discussions and making great content so your subscribers see the value in what you're doing. Whatever you do, don't turn the group into a spammy sales fest. This can make a big difference to your churn because once people make connections and feel like they are part of something, it prevents them from cancelling.

- **Create a Blog** – Make a blog and write as many relevant, helpful, and interesting articles as possible about your niche, then regularly promote it to your customers. If you provide genuine value to people, they are less likely to cancel.
- **Go live and answer questions** – Set a date with your subscribers for when you plan to go live on Facebook. Make it an event and tell them you will be answering as many questions as possible about your business. You should do this regularly, and it will help build community and reduce churn.

5. Reward programs

Set up a reward program. E.g. a customer will receive a free item, or they will get a discount after so many boxes. You should set it like this three boxes, six boxes, twelve boxes etc. Make sure the rewards are good enough so customers will look forward to receiving them.

You can also do one better by doing a big monthly raffle. Tell all your active subscribers they are entered into it and then go live on Facebook at a set time of the month. Make it a fun experience and give away some decent prizes. This will get your entire subscriber base involved and help increase customer loyalty.

6. Learn the points where a customer is most likely to churn and reach out before they do it

A SaaS company has an advantage when it comes to this point. They are able to analyse their user's behaviour and understand when somebody is likely to churn. E.g. They haven't logged in for a certain period of time, or they don't use a certain feature. If they see a customer fall into this behaviour pattern, they can reach out to the customer and try and save them before they churn. (Trust me, it is much easier to save somebody than it is to try and get them to sign up again) We don't have this luxury with a subscription box business, but we can do the next best thing. The next best thing would be to monitor your monthly cohorts and try and understand at what point in a customer's subscription are their spikes in churn. Once you know this information, you can then put processes in place to intercept them and try and save them.

E.g., Here's an example.

You look at your monthly cohorts, and you notice between month one and month two, there is a big spike in churn. You survey these customers, and you come to the conclusion they are leaving because they don't really understand your service and they don't think it is right for them. You then put a plan in place to engage with future customers during this point of their subscription and try and save them. You can either do this by email, or what I find works really well is getting your support staff to call them and ask how they are doing and what they think of the service.

You need to be very creative when fighting your churn rate, and sometimes you also must be willing to incentivise your customers to stay. Some people struggle with this because they feel like they are losing money when they go with this approach. My advice is to check your lifetime value, and once you understand that, you will know what kind of incentives you can give.

CHAPTER 13
Other Subscription Box Metrics

One of the biggest reasons why we have been able to create so much success in BusterBox is that we place a massive emphasis on tracking and improving our subscription metrics. There are a few different metrics which are vital to any subscription business. These metrics will give you a clear understanding of how healthy your business is. In this chapter, I am going to break down all of them and explain to you why you should be monitoring them and how you can improve them to ensure you are on the right path.

I take a look at our metrics first thing every morning in BusterBox. I log into our software which displays all this information and I go through everything. This helps me to understand if we are going in the right direction or do we need to make some adjustments on our journey. I encourage you to do the same in your subscription business. If you don't know any of this information, how can you possibly know if you are on the right path?

I have spent a lot of time reading and learning about subscription metrics from a SaaS founder's perspective. I find it very interesting that SaaS founders spend so much time analysing and working on their metrics compared to many Subscription Box founders. This doesn't make sense to me because, at the end of the day, both business models are subscription based. Yes, SaaS founders provide access to software for their customers, and Subscription Box founders deliver physical products, but both business models generate revenue through subscriptions. This means there is a lot of cross-over regarding metrics, and you should take this stuff very seriously if you want to be successful.

Here are the names of different software that can track your metrics

- ChartMogul
- Baremetrics
- Profit Well
- Sublytics

By the end of this chapter, you will be an expert on all kinds of subscription metrics. Your knowledge on the topic will be miles ahead of the majority of business owners in the subscription box industry.

So let's jump straight into it.

1. Customer Lifetime Value

This is how much each customer gives you on average throughout the lifetime of their subscription. I am going to be very blunt here. If you have been operating for over a year and you still don't understand your customer's lifetime value, you shouldn't be running any form of paid advertising. You shouldn't be doing this because you don't know what a customer is worth to you, so you don't know how much you can even spend to acquire a new customer.

This is why a large proportion of Subscription Box companies struggle to turn a profit. Either they are spending way too much on customer recruitment versus lifetime value, or they aren't spending enough.

I have witnessed the second point happen multiple times for new Subscription Box founders. They have found a profitable marketing channel, but they are afraid to increase their marketing budget to acquire customers quicker because they are unsure of how it will directly impact their business.

This leaves them in limbo where they aren't hitting their growth targets, and they haven't enough subscribers signed up to turn a profit when all they need to do to solve this problem is increase the marketing budget and get more subscribers signed up, but the lack of clarity around their Subscription Box metrics is killing their business.

As mentioned previously, you should be using software to calculate this to know your information is accurate.

This is how you would calculate it manually, though, just so you know.

Example:

1. Your average revenue per user is $20 (This is what your average box costs across all plans)
2. Your monthly churn rate is 10% (customers stay ten months)
3. Multiply $20 by ten months

4. Lifetime value = $200
5. Of course, this is a very basic calculation and doesn't account for any discount you may apply at the start of the subscription.

Here's a tip

A customer's lifetime value doesn't have to end once they cancel their subscription. So if you are smart, you will sell your email list once-off products. This is a fantastic way to boost a customer's lifetime value and maximize the amount of cash you make from every customer.

2. Gross Margin As Part Of Lifetime Value

Here's another part that needs to be addressed. The lifetime value I discussed above only accounts for revenue. To truly understand how much a customer is worth, you need to consider your gross margin. Gross margin is the amount of money left over after taking out the costs required to send a box.

Here's a simple way to work it out

1. Company A makes $18 gross profit per box
2. The typical customer stays signed up for twelve months
3. $18 X twelve months = $216
4. Company A makes an average profit of $216 for each customer.

When working out this calculation, ensure you include every single cost in delivering a box to a customer. That includes products, cardboard, shipping, inserts, payment fees, etc. Everything needs to be included so you clearly understand exactly how much profit you are making on average for each customer.

3. LTV: CAC Ratio

This is one of the key metrics that will help you determine if the business you are building will be a success or if you are just sending your cash up in smoke. You should be aiming to have your LTV: CAC Ratio at 3:1 as a minimum target. This would mean you earn back three times, on average, the amount of money you spend to acquire a customer.

Example 1

On average, it costs you $30 on Facebook ads to acquire a customer.
You are earning 10$ gross profit on each box.
You keep customers signed up for nine months on average.
Nine months X $10 = $90.
This means you earn $90 profit on average from each customer.
90 / 30 = 3
Your LTV: CAC Ratio is 3:1
E.g. you earn back three times what you spend to acquire customers.

Now let me give you another example.

Example 2

Imagine it costs you $50 to get a customer signed up from Facebook Ads.
You are earning $5 gross profit on each box.
You keep customers signed up for ten months on average.

10 months x $5 = $50
This means you earn $50 profit on average from each customer.
But in this example, getting somebody signed up costs you $50.

So you actually earn no profit at all throughout the lifetime of each subscription, and to make matters worse, you are losing money as you still need to pay all the costs required to run your business.

These two examples demonstrate why the LTV: CAC Ratio is such an important metric when running any subscription business. If you want to raise money from any VC or an experienced investor, this is one of the first metrics they will ask for. If you are able to tell them you have a strong LTV: CAC Ratio, there is a much higher chance they will invest in your company as they know your business is sustainable and has the ability to support growth. If you get back to them with a poor LTV: CAC Ratio, they will run away from your business as fast as their legs will carry them. This is because they know your business doesn't make any financial sense, and it doesn't matter what level you get to. You will always be burning cash.

In the SAAS world, they say a 3:1 ratio is ideal and that's what everybody should be aiming for. They say if the ratio is any higher, you are probably leaving money on the table and you are not aggressive enough with your marketing because there are probably more customers you could be signing up. In my experience, when it comes to Subscription Boxes, you want to aim to have as high of a ratio as possible, and 3:1 is the minimum you should be aiming for. You should still be hitting your growth goals and getting a good volume of customers signed up, but the higher you can get, the more profitable your business will be.

4. Average Revenue Per User (ARPU)

The average revenue per user (ARPU) Is the revenue generated (on average) by each active subscriber signed up to your box. This is a very helpful metric which will enable you to understand how much revenue all your different subscription plans generate for your business when added together.

I will give you an example:

It is highly unlikely you will be running a subscription box business with only one plan and one price. Instead, you are probably going to have multiple subscriptions, which all have different prices.

E.g. Your 6-month, 12-month and 1-month should all be priced differently. Then if you are offering upgrades to those subscriptions, you will also have other plans priced differently. Your ARPU will account for all the different plans and prices and show you, on average, what each active subscriber is worth to your business every month.

Your ARPU can be calculated by dividing the total revenue generated during a month by the total number of active users during the same time period.

For example, if you generated $100,00 last month and had three thousand active subscribers that month, Your Average Revenue Per User would be $33.33.

You should be tracking this metric and always looking to improve it.

Our ARPU in BusterBox today is much higher than when we originally started the business. We managed to increase it by raising our prices across all of our subscription plans and also including upgrades customers can add to their subscriptions. This is a work in progress and we are always testing new upgrades to see how high we can get this too. If you have a higher ARPU, you will have a higher Customer Lifetime value which means your business will be more profitable and you can spend more on marketing to acquire more customers.

5. Monthly Recurring Revenue

Your monthly recurring revenue (MRR) represents the total revenue generated by your business from all of your active subscriptions in a particular month. It includes discounts and recurring add-ons but does not include one-time – fees.

You can use your MRR as a quick way to indicate your business's financial health and project future earnings based on active subscriptions.

This is one of the first metrics I check each morning as it gives me a quick view of the company and lets me understand if we are growing or if we are losing revenue.

How To Calculate MRR?

Calculating your MRR is very easy. All you need to do is multiply the number of monthly subscribers by the average revenue per user (ARPU)

Example:

You have three hundred active subscribers and your average revenue per user is $25

(300x$25) = $7500

Expansion MRR:

Your expansion MRR is a portion of your company's MRR which is attributed to additional revenue generated from existing customers.

Examples

- **Upselling:** Your customers upgrade to a more expensive version of your box.
- **Cross—Selling:** Your customers purchase another subscription through your company. E.g. you have a dog subscription box and start offering a cat subscription box, and some of your existing customers sign up for it.
- **Add–Ons:** Customers pay for additional recurring add-ons, e.g. extra products or access to digital products.

Expansion MRR can be a powerful way of growing the monthly revenue in your company with little to no marketing costs.

Example: We launched a dog food subscription to our existing customers. There was zero marketing budget spent on this launch. All we did was email and call existing customers. We ended up substantially growing our MRR by doing this.

I have witnessed many different subscription companies try to increase MRR with expansion revenue, and it usually works well once you understand your customers and know what they actually want. However, the biggest mistake you can make when it comes to this is when you don't have a clue what your customers want, and you end up launching another product to try and grow your expansion revenue, and it completely flops.

Launching a new product, even if it is only designed to increase your expansion revenue, takes time and resources, so before you jump in, make sure you do your research first.

6. Annual Run Rate (ARR)

Your Annual Run Rate is your yearly version of your MRR. Your ARR will help you project your future revenue for the next twelve months based on your current MRR. It assumes nothing will change in the next twelve months. That means no churn, no new customers, and no expansion revenue. This is obviously unrealistic, as all those things will happen in your business, but ARR is still a helpful way of predicting long-term growth.

When you hear people talking about having a $1 million business, they usually mean they have $1 million ARR. This means they are set to bring in $1 million in recurring revenue in the next twelve months at the rate they are going.

It is easy to calculate your ARR. All you need to do is multiply your MRR by twelve. For example, if your MRR for last month were $50,000, Your ARR would be $600,000.

One of our biggest goals in BusterBox was to get our MRR to $84,000 because I knew once we hit that, our ARR would surpass $1 million, and we would have a million-dollar business. When we eventually achieved this goal, knowing we had built a million-dollar business from nothing was very satisfying. We have since surpassed this by a lot, but the memory of hitting the first million will always stand out to me. I encourage you to pay attention to this metric in your business and set goals around it. I have found it is a great way to motivate you to keep growing.

7. Subscription Payback Period

Your subscription payback period is the average amount of time it takes for your customers to become profitable. So when you are running paid traffic and scaling, there is a good chance your new customers won't be profitable straight away. This is absolutely fine as you are running a Subscription business, so you don't need them to be profitable immediately.

Now in an ideal world, you want to make sure your subscription payback period is as short as possible. Otherwise, the cash flow in your business will be a mess, and you will need a lot of investment to grow your customer base. In my experience, an acceptable Payback period for a direct-to-consumer subscription is 3 – 4 months max. If it is any longer, it will be challenging to bootstrap the business.

A shorter payback period will improve the amount of cash you have on hand in your business. This means you can grow faster as you have more cash to reinvest in marketing and acquiring more customers. Your payback period should be tracked throughout the lifetime of your business, as it helps paint a picture of what your long-term profitability will look like. Also, suppose you are looking to sell your business or raise a round of investment. In that case, your Payback period will help determine how attractive the deal is for a potential buyer or investor.

You can calculate your Payback period with this simple formula

Just divide the cost of acquiring a new customer by the gross profit you earn from each box.

Example

It costs you $50 to get somebody signed up for your box. You are earning $10 gross profit on each box. So in five months, that customer will have repaid the cost of acquiring them.

$50 CAC / $10 profit per month = 5 months.

Now one thing you must remember is that this formula does not account for customer churn. So what happens if a percentage of those customer's churn before you hit the 5-month mark? The marketing cost to get those customers has already been spent and will remain the same, but the amount of revenue they generate will be reduced.

This means the average payback period in your business will increase.

The best way to solve this is to remove all the customers who churned out of the equation and calculate their loss completely separately.

How to Reduce Your Payback Period

You can do a few different things to reduce the payback period in your business. The most obvious solution would either be to reduce your customer acquisition cost or improve the gross profit you earn on each subscription. If you do either of those things, you will reduce the payback period, and customers will be in profit faster. Now, the issue is. It isn't always possible to do either of those things in every business. Sometimes, the CAC is what it is, and despite all the testing in the world, you can't find a way to lower it. Or you have hit a price barrier in your business, and it isn't possible to improve your gross profit any further on each box. When you find yourself in these situations, you need to get very creative with your approach to reducing your payback period.

Here are a few different things that you can test.

1. **Increase Your Average Order Value (AOV)**

Increasing your average order value is a great way to reduce your payback period. When you increase your average order value, Customers pay you more on the initial transaction when they first sign up. When you earn more profit, it decreases the amount of time it takes to turn a customer profitable. The best way to increase your average order value is to include upsells in your sales process. At the end of the day, you know what your customers are interested in, so it should not be that difficult to offer them more products they are likely to be tempted to buy.

I will give you an example.

One of the post-purchase upsells we offer in BusterBox is a dog bed. This is something that every dog owner is tempted to buy, as there is a good chance that the old bed will need to be replaced now or at some point soon. This has a very high uptake and we make a good margin on it, so it helps us to boost our AOV and reduce our payback period.

We have also included past dog toy and treat bundles, collars, leads, and dog grooming kits. All of these have sold well as post-purchase upsells at different points.

If you don't offer any upsells in your business, you are 100% leaving money on the table. I highly recommend testing as many different products and bundles as possible to learn what will have the highest uptake and make you the most money.

I have an easy solution for you if you don't know what other items your customers are buying. Just survey them and ask. That's what we did and continue to do in Busterbox. Let your customers tell you what they want and then simply give it to them. That is a winning combo that never fails.

A great post-purchase upsell, which I have witnessed work time and time again in many different niches, is a mystery box.

Let me explain how it works.

If you have old boxes or stock you want to get rid of, you can turn them into a "Mystery Box." You then allow your customers to purchase this "Mystery Box" as a post-purchase upsell. It works very well because it is a bit of fun, and customers become curious about what could potentially be found in this "Mystery Box." If you decide to do this, please ensure the box you send out has good quality products in it and is worth the value the customer paid. The quickest way to destroy the trust of a new subscriber is by trying to rip them off and send out crap. If you do this right, though, you will have a high uptake, and it will help a lot to raise your AOV.

2. Sell Subscription On The Back End

Another great way to reduce your Payback period is by selling your subscription box on the back end of your funnel.

Let me explain how that works.

You could create a digital product which fits in nicely with the niche of your box. Once that product is created, you would then sell it.

Example:

- You own a dog subscription box.
- You decide to create a digital dog training product.
- You sell that product for $47 (Because it is a digital product, you make nearly a 100% margin on it)
- You start running ads for this product and get your customer acquisition cost down to $30.
- After somebody signs up, sell your subscription box as a post-purchase upsell.
- Now instead of having a payback period and paying for customers to join your box, you are making a $15 - $17 profit on the first transaction.
- You have entirely eliminated your payback period.

This can be a challenge to get working, depending on your niche. If you manage to pull it off, though, it can work like magic, and you can grow your box quickly with little investment as the payback period has been reduced or essentially doesn't exist anymore. I would recommend having a think and then trying to figure out how you can add a funnel like this to your business.

3. Testing Different Marketing Channels

Not all marketing channels will cost the same to acquire a customer. So you should track your CAC across every channel and then focus on the ones that give you the cheapest and best return. Be careful not to analyse a marketing channel from CAC alone, though. If the CAC is low and the volume is low, that will not help you. Likewise, if the CAC is low, but the quality of customers is terrible, and you get high churn, that isn't going to help either.

The ideal combination is low CAC, high volume, and good quality customers. So that is why you need to track CAC, volume, and LTV, and once you find the channels that tick all those boxes, you should put your foot down and go all in on them.

CHAPTER 14
Subscription Break–Even Point

If you have been running your subscription box for a while, you probably wonder when you will start making good money from your business. Or you might be a brand new subscription box entrepreneur and you are trying to forecast when you will be able to leave your job and start earning a full-time income from your subscription box. Well, the answer to both of those questions is the exact same thing. You will start seeing a profit when you pass the break-even point in your business.

In BusterBox myself and the two other founders became utterly obsessed with our break-even point from very early on. We wanted to know exactly how many subscribers we needed and what our monthly revenue had to be to have a healthy business where we could get paid, pay our staff, and have enough money to keep growing.

I think this is very important, and every subscription box business should spend some time working this out. Only then will you know what the goal is and you will be able to calculate the amount of time and money it will take to get there.

So what is the definition of a break–even point in a business?

The break-even point is the point at which total cost and revenue are equal, meaning there is no loss or gain for your business. In other words, you are producing enough profit to cover your costs and no longer losing money.

The above statement is pulled directly from Google and is 100% correct. Once you surpass the breakeven point, you will start producing profit in your business.

So what is the quickest way to work out your break–even point?

The first thing you need to work out is your gross margin. E.g., the amount of profit you make on each box after you fill it, package it, and ship it out to the customer.

Next, you should write down a list of all the fixed costs in your business. Your fixed costs are essential to running your business and you know the cost won't change as you scale.

Example

- Software
- Insurance
- Warehouse Rent
- Loan repayments
- Annual Staff salaries

Go through your bank statements carefully and ensure you have everything listed. This is a good opportunity to cancel what isn't 100% needed. Now add up the exact amount you spend on your fixed cost each month and write this figure down.

You now need to go through your variable costs and do the same thing. Your variable costs can change monthly, but you should still have a rough idea of what they will be. So go through them and write them down.

Example

- Software (with transaction fees)
- Credit card fees
- Staff salaries which are paid by the hour.

Once you have done that, add up your fixed and variable costs and see how much they cost per month. Once you know that figure, you can work out how many boxes you need to ship per month to cover it and reach the break-even point. Now you may think that is it, but because we are running a subscription box business, we have some other stuff we have to account for. The next bit of information is vital and is where many subscription boxes struggle, so they never go profitable.

As discussed, some key metrics play a big part in how profitable your Subscription Box business will be. I will explain how they affect your break-even point.

These are the metrics

CPA (Cost Per Acquisition)

Monthly Churn Rate

MRR — Monthly Recurring Revenue

ARPU — Average Revenue Per User
Customer Lifetime Value

Case Study.

Now let's come up with an imaginary subscription box and do a case study to see its break-even point. BasketBall Box is a monthly delivery of Basketball goodies straight to your door.

Fixed Costs

Including annual salaries and everything mentioned above, this comes up to $12,000 per month

Variable Costs

These currently cost about $2,000, per month but are likely to rise once the company grows.

Metrics

BasketBall box is $30 per month and they make $10 gross profit per box

Their monthly churn rate is 10%. This means they keep the average person signed up for ten months and they make $100 gross profit throughout the lifetime of the subscription.

It costs them $12.50 to get a new customer signed up

Summary

Not including marketing costs, they need to make $14,000, gross profit per month to keep the lights on. This works out at fourteen hundred subscribers.

If they don't spend any money on marketing though the business will collapse so that really isn't an option, they need to be replacing customers at a minimum each month.

So at fourteen hundred subscribers with 10% churn, they need to replace a hundred and forty customers each month.

We worked out their CPA is $12.50, so multiply that by a hundred and forty and you get $1,750 spent on marketing per month.

This means in total, they need roughly $15,750 in gross profit each month to break even.

This equals one thousand five hundred and seventy-five active subscribers.

This is a very rough example and can get a lot more complicated.

These numbers were made up from thin air. If you do this calculation again and increase the churn by 5% and the CPA by $5, it will make a difference to the break-even point.

I also kept it simple and never mentioned anything about future growth. The dream for all subscription box companies is to hit the break-even point and then be able to fund future growth through their revenues. I also never mentioned anything about taxes, how other costs can come into the picture, or a number of other factors, including cash flow.

I hope this breakdown gives you a clear idea of what you need to do to work out the break-even point in your business so you can start earning some real money.

Obviously, the break-even point is never set exactly in stone, and it can fluctuate a bit in a subscription business because of the metrics. However, you should still follow this formula to clearly understand what level you need to grow your business to reach it.

I also never mentioned selling any other products on the back end, which is essential and will help you earn more money from each customer and hit the break-even point quicker. It amazes me in the Subscription Box industry how so many business owners do not have a clue of what their breakeven point is and how they plan to actually get there. If you don't know what you're aiming for regarding subscriber count and revenue goals, you will likely keep running around in circles and burning money in the process.

When you fully understand your breakeven point, you can put together a plan and take the necessary steps to reach it. Then once you surpass it, you can start producing healthy profits regularly.

CHAPTER 15
Create Your Dream Subscription Box Business

Over the course of this book, I have broken down exactly what you need to do to start and grow a highly profitable subscription box. You now have all the tools and the blueprint for making your dreams a reality. The sad thing is, I know a large percentage of people who read this will never do what is necessary to build a successful business. You can read all the books in the world, but if you aren't an action-taker, you won't get anywhere. The majority of people will either never finish the book or they will finish it but won't bother to do anything with any of the information.

Please do not be one of those people.

If you have reached this point in the book, you have consumed all the information you need to build your dream subscription box business. Your next step is putting the book down and taking action immediately. Please do not come up with excuses or say that now is not the right time to start a business. I will let you in on a little secret. There is never a right time to start a business. There will always be something at any point in your life that you can use as an excuse to stop you from taking action.

When we started BusterBox it was 100% not the right time for me. I was in debt from my last business that failed and I was just about to start college for the second time while working full-time. I didn't let any of that stop me, though. I wanted to change my life and I was ready to do everything in my power to make it happen. I decided to quit college after two days and I jumped straight into building BusterBox. A few years later, all my debt is repaid and I own a business that has done millions in sales.

I can tell you now none of this was easy, but I would do it all again in a flash if I had to. Apart from the financial rewards, there is something extremely satisfying about building your own company and controlling your destiny. It doesn't make a difference if you are planning on building a multimillion-dollar subscription box business that you plan to exit one day or if you simply want to start a side hustle that can give you some spare cash. The opportunity is there with this business model; it is up to you to seize it and change your life.

When you are getting started, you should have a clear goal of how you want your business and your life to look. When you do this, you are giving yourself a clear target to aim for. Then you simply reverse-engineer all the steps you need to take to achieve the goal. Some people want to scale to hundreds of thousands of subscribers and have a big exit. Others want to create a lifestyle business and some people only want to create a side hustle that earns them some more money on top of their salary each month. There is nothing wrong with any of these options. All of them can turn out great. It just depends on the person and what they actually want to achieve. No matter what option you choose, though, here are some essential things every subscription box needs to provide.

1. Healthy Salary

This is something that I believe every single business owner deserves and is actually essential. You have taken a lot of risks setting up your business and have put yourself under a lot of stress, so the minimum thing you need in return from your business is a healthy salary. When you first start your business, it is perfectly normal to work without any salary for a period of time. I would recommend you keep your job at this point and work on your business in the evenings and weekends. Then when you see your business is starting to build up momentum and cash flow, you can quit your job. During this period, you may not be generating enough from your business to fully replace your old salary, but you should have cash saved up to help for a few months.

When you get to this point, you have decided to go all in on your business and you should focus on it 100% and do everything in your power to get it to the level where it fully replaces your salary. I fully believe every single person who has any kind of positive traction in their subscription box can get to this point with the right strategy and effort. You just have to understand the maths and not underestimate the consistent effort that it will take.

2. Freedom

At some point in your subscription box business, you will want to achieve a level of freedom. Obviously, when you are starting out, hard work is a requirement, and you will need to dedicate a lot of time if you want to get anywhere. I am afraid there is no way around that, but eventually, the idea is to get your freedom back, earn more money and have a much better quality of life. I think this is a pretty fair trade-off. You sacrifice a period of time and focus 100% on your business to ensure you have a much better future.

The only way you will be able to achieve this though, is by having your business in a position where you can afford to hire a team to help out with tasks. The good news is it isn't that difficult to hire people to take over some key tasks which take up a lot of time.

The two main areas which need to be covered as soon as possible are the following.

- **Fulfilment**
- **Customer Service**

These are the big-time sinks in most Subscription Box Businesses. When you are starting out, it is important you do the customer service yourself to connect with your customers and ensure processes are put in place. This isn't sustainable, though. As you grow, this will eat more and more into your productive hours and will start affecting the overall performance of your company.

Customer service is not a hard role to fill. You can hire virtual assistants that can do a great job. You just have to ensure you interview them correctly and provide them with good training and support so they can do the job to a high standard. Then, once your business gets bigger, you will be in a position to hire more help who can help with some other tasks.

It is down to you as a business owner to understand what areas you need help with. This will be different for everyone.

Here are some suggestions.

- Paid Traffic
- Sourcing Products
- Finances
- Social media
- Content Creation
- Data Analyst
- Graphic Design

I think most people will agree if you get paid well and you have the freedom to spend time with your family, you have a pretty good life and that's what you should strive for as a minimum in your business. Now to get to this point in your business, you need to have a plan, and you need to know at what point this will be possible for you.

The Plan To Reverse Engineer Your Dream Business.
I am a big fan of reverse engineering things because, in my mind, it lays out a path that you can follow to achieve your goal. If you have been running your Subscription Box for a while and feel like you aren't making any progress, this is the point you should stop, do this exercise, and reassess things. You will then have the clarity you need to get to this point.

Like I have said so many times, the entire game is based on maths and if you can get the numbers to work in your favour everything will be a million times easier.
The first thing you need to do is to work out how much money you need to be earning every month to live your dream life. Once you know what this figure is then, you can reverse engineer your entire business to hit this figure.

I will show you an example from a fantasy Subscription Box Company I just made up.
Let's call them Football Box.

The founder of Football Box worked out that if they were earning $8000 per month, they would be living their dream life. $8000 per month would be a higher salary than they ever earned in any previous job. This would allow them to buy their dream home, take care of their family, give them the freedom to travel regularly, and enable them to have full financial security.

Once the founder of Football box realised $8000 per month was the number they needed, they then went ahead and started reverse engineering the entire process to hit that number.

Here are the monthly expenses of the business

1. **Software costs – $600 P.M**
2. **Warehouse Cost – $800 P.M**
3. **Salary – $8,000 P.M**
4. **Staff Salary – $4,000 P.M**
5. **Other Expenses $1,500 P.M**

If you add all of these numbers up, you can see this company needs to generate $14,900 per month in gross profit to stay in business.

Now let's take a look at their COGS and Subscription Metrics to understand how big the business needs to be to give the founder their dream life.

The average revenue per user across all subscribers is $50 per month.

The gross margin of Football Box is 50%

This means they earn $25 profit on each box. (This is after everything is paid. Cardboard, shipping, products, payment gateways, etc.)

To generate $14,900 in gross profit each month, they only need 596 active subscribers.

When you put it into perspective that really isn't a lot at all.

The only issue is we haven't factored in churn or marketing costs, so let's add these in and see how it looks.

Football Box has an average churn rate of 10% each month and their CPA to get a new customer is $20

This means out of the five hundred ninety-six active subscribers they need, they are losing around sixty customers a month to cancellations, and it is costing them $1,200 per month to replace them (60 x $20 = $1,200)
So let's factor that into the costs that we just worked out.

To generate enough money to cover all the bills and their marketing costs, they need around six hundred forty–four active subscribers.
Honestly, think about that 644 active subscribers are all the business needs so the founder can create their dream life. Obviously, this is a very rough calculation again, but it gives you a very good idea of how this imaginary founder would reverse engineer the situation to reach their goal.

644 x $25 = $16,100 gross profit generated each month

The founder will earn an $8,000 salary per month.

There are other employees working in the company, so the founder isn't run into the ground, and all expenses are paid for.

Six hundred forty-four is not a lot of subscribers and it is 100% possible for this business to get these people signed up pretty quickly. Football is very popular and the market is big enough to support this business. As this business grows, the founder will be able to increase their salary, hire more help, bank more profit for the business and reinvest money into marketing which will help them grow even quicker.

Just imagine Football Box with 2,000 active subscribers

They would be generating $50,000 per month in gross profit

Two thousand subscribers may seem like a lot, but honestly, once you get the marketing sorted, it is not that many people. If you want to really turn your Subscription Box into something that can completely change your life, I urge you to do the exact same exercise that I just did in your own business. You need to decide what your ideal number is. Then once you understand the maths, you will then have clarity about the steps you need to take to reverse engineer your dream business/life.

You should attack this goal extremely aggressively and do everything in your power to reach it ASAP. You now have the power and the knowledge to completely change your life, so please don't let yourself down by not even trying. You will be surprised by the amount of work you can get done and the progress you can make when you have a clear goal to aim for.

If I can build a multimillion-dollar subscription box business from scratch with no connections and barely any money, then you can do the same. I hope you found this book valuable and wish you the best of luck on your journey. The subscription box business model completely changed my life and can also change yours.

FREE Subscription Box Training $399 Value

First of all, CONGRATULATIONS for investing in "The Subscription Box Blueprint"! As a token of our appreciation, we have an EXCLUSIVE gift for you.

Introducing: "Scale to 10,000 Subscribers & Beyond"

A FREE Masterclass Valued at $399, Just for You!

This is the same masterclass that I presented live at the SubSummit conference in Orlando as an extra-paid workshop. And now, it's yours for **FREE** as our special gift to you!

Here's what you'll discover in this exclusive FREE masterclass:

- The exact strategies and tactics that helped us scale BusterBox to 10,000 subscribers and beyond
- Insider secrets that I've used to help countless subscription boxes in every niche you can possibly think of scale up to new levels
- Proven marketing techniques that will keep your customers coming back for more, month after month
- Lessons from the trenches of building and scaling successful subscription box businesses

To claim your exclusive FREE masterclass, simply follow these steps:

- Head over to www.thesubscriptionboxblueprint.com/freegift or scan the QR code included on this page.
- Enter your name and email address to get instant access.

SCAN THIS QR CODE TO ACCESS THE FREE MASTERCLASS

SCAN THIS CODE TO ACCESS THE FREE MASTERCLASS

Boom! That's it! By entering your email, you'll unlock instant access to the "Scale to 10,000 Subscribers & Beyond" masterclass. Not only that, but you'll also join our exclusive tribe of subscription box entrepreneurs and receive valuable insights, tips, and resources sent straight to your inbox.

Glossary

Alibaba: A Chinese multinational conglomerate holding company specializing in e-commerce, retail, Internet, and technology.

AliExpress: This is an online retail service owned by Alibaba Group. It is a platform that allows small businesses in China to sell their products to customers around the world, and it is often compared to Amazon. Aliexpress offers a wide range of products, from clothing and accessories to electronics and home goods.

Amazon: Amazon is an American multinational technology company based in Seattle, Washington. It is one of the world's largest online retailers and provides a wide range of products and services, including electronics, books, household goods, and streaming services. Amazon also offers services like cloud computing, artificial intelligence, and digital advertising. You can source products through amazon and also sell your Subscription Box through Amazon.

Active Campaign: This is a software company that provides a range of marketing and sales automation tools. The company's platform offers email marketing, marketing automation, and customer relationship management (CRM) solutions, among other features.

Average Order Value: (AOV) is a metric used in e-commerce to measure the average amount of money that a customer spends on a single purchase on a website or online platform.

Annual Run Rate: ARR is your yearly version of MRR. Your ARR will help you project your future revenue for the next 12 months based on current MRR.

Average Revenue Per User (ARPU) is a measure of the revenue generated by a business for each individual user. In the context of a subscription box business, ARPU can be calculated by dividing the total revenue generated from subscriptions by the number of subscribers.

Active Users: In the context of a subscription box service, active users refer to the number of customers who are currently subscribed to the service and receiving regular deliveries of products.

Active Churn: This is also known as customer churn it is a measure of the number of customers who stop using a product or service over a given period of time. In the context of a subscription box service, active churn refers to the number of customers who cancel their subscriptions and no longer receive regular deliveries of products.

Bounce Rate: This metric measures the percentage of website visitors who leave a website after viewing only one page.

Bold Subscriptions: This is a subscription box platform which can be used to manage your subscriptions and run your business.

Baremetrics: Software to keep track of all your subscription metrics

Cold Traffic: In marketing, cold traffic refers to potential customers who have not had any previous interaction with a business or its products or services.

CrateJoy: This is a subscription box platform that allows businesses to create and manage their own subscription box services. The platform provides tools and resources for businesses to design and customize their subscription boxes, manage customer relationships, and process orders and payments.

ChartMogul: Software to keep track of all your subscription metrics

CAC: Customer acquisition cost is how much it costs to sign up a new subscriber to your box.

CPA: Cost per action is how much it costs for a potential customer to perform the desired action. E.g. become a subscriber. (Just another way of phrasing your customer acquisition cost)

Churn: Subscription box churn refers to the number of customers who cancel their subscriptions to a subscription box service over a given period of time. This metric is important for subscription box businesses, as it provides insight into the effectiveness of their retention efforts and can help identify areas for improvement.

Conversion Rate: This metric measures the percentage of website visitors who take a desired action, such as making a purchase or filling out a form, during their visit. It is calculated by dividing the number of conversions (or desired actions) by the total number of website visitors and expressing the result as a percentage.

Cut–off date/point: This is the last date a new customer can subscribe for the current subscription box

COGS: Cost of goods sold. The total cost to sell a box including products, cardboard, fulfilment, shipping etc..

Call to action: This is the action you want a customer to take. E.g. Buy your box, join your email list etc..

Direct response marketing: – This Marketing is a type of advertising that seeks to elicit an immediate response from consumers, such as making a purchase or contacting the business to learn more about a product or service. This is in contrast to more traditional forms of advertising, which are primarily focused on building brand awareness and recognition over time.

Digital Product: This is a type of product that is delivered and consumed in a digital format. Examples of digital products include software, ebooks, online courses, music and video files, and digital images. Digital products can be downloaded or accessed online and do not have a physical form. The best thing about them is that they have a very high margin.

Email Marketing: This is a form of digital marketing that involves sending marketing messages or advertisements to a group of people through email.

Etsy: An e-commerce website that focuses on handmade or vintage items and supplies, as well as unique factory-manufactured items. It is a platform that allows artists, craftspeople, and collectors to sell their items online.

Fulfilment Center: This is a third-party vendor who stores your products, packs your boxes and ships them to your subscribers.

Facebook Ads: This is a digital advertising platform developed by Facebook that allows businesses to display ads on the Facebook and Instagram platforms.

Gross Profit: Gross profit is the profit that a company makes after deducting the cost of goods sold (COGS) from its revenue. It is a measure of the profitability of a company's core business operations, and it is calculated by subtracting the COGS from the total revenue.

Google Ads: (formerly known as Google AdWords) is a digital advertising platform developed by Google that allows businesses to display ads on Google and its advertising network.

Influencer Marketing: This is a type of digital marketing that involves partnering with individuals who have a large following on social media or other online platforms, and who are seen as trusted sources of information and recommendations by their followers. These individuals, known as influencers, promote products or services to their followers through sponsored posts, reviews, or other forms of content.

KPI: Key performance indicators are metrics that are used to measure how different areas of the business are performing.

Lifetime Value: LTV is the total amount of revenue that a customer is expected to generate over the lifetime of their subscription.

LTV: CAC Ratio: The LTV / CAC Ratio compares the value of a customer over their lifetime to the cost of acquiring them. You should be aiming to hit a 3:1 ratio as a minimum.

Monthly Recurring Revenue: Your MRR represents the total revenue generated by your business from all of your active subscriptions in a particular month.

Niche: A small specific category within a market.

Net Profit: Also known as net income or net earnings, is a measure of a company's profitability. It represents the amount of money that a company has made after accounting for all of its expenses, including the cost of goods sold, operating expenses, and taxes. Net profit is calculated by subtracting total expenses from total revenue.

Offer: To break it down in its simplest form, a Subscription Box offer is what you give a consumer in exchange for signing up for your box. An offer doesn't only have to involve discounting prices you can also bundle things together to entice the consumer to take action and purchase your box.

Paid advertising: Paid advertising refers to using paid media channels to promote a product, service, or brand to a target audience. Examples would be Facebook ads or Google ads.

Payback Period: The number of payments it takes to turn a subscriber profitable.

Pre–Launch: This is the marketing you do before you launch your subscription box. It helps you to create awareness of your product, build some anticipation and buzz around the launch and generate some viable leads.

Profitwell: Software to keep track of all your subscription metrics

Procurement: Sourcing products that will be included in your subscription box.

Recurring Payments: These are payments that come through repeatedly without selling any additional products. With a subscription box, it is common to have all your subscribers pay you automatically each month.

Retention Rate: The percentage of subscribers who remain subscribed to your subscription box.

Recharge: This is a subscription box platform which can be used to manage your subscriptions and run your business.

Sales Funnel: This is a web page that is designed to turn a potential customer into a buyer. Most funnels will have components such as a sales page/ order form, multiple upsells and a thank you page. When it comes to a subscription box business, using a sales funnel can be a good strategy to help you earn back your ad spend as quickly as possible.

Subbly: This is a subscription box platform which can be used to manage your subscriptions and run your business.

SEO: Search engine optimization. This is when you use specific techniques to increase your traffic and raise your website's visibility in search engines.

Warm Traffic: This is a group of people who are aware of your brand but they have not yet made a purchase.

Printed in Great Britain
by Amazon

28431174R00129